To Tony,

It is great meeting you
I know that this Book
will help you Grow!

Words of Praise for *The Art of Communication*

"*THE ART OF COMMUNICATION* serves as a "How To" for a variety of interactions...as a business owner; I face potential obstacles in interaction with clients, vendors and colleagues every day. In addition, the tools set forth in the book can be easily implemented into everyday social interactions...as a husband and father, communication is of utmost importance and The Art of Communication is a valuable asset in navigating the complex map of effective expression.

Bravo to Yohance for his foray into published work and for overcoming the challenges life presented to him...this project is a result of a proven, organic and cultivated system that Yohance applied to himself before presenting to his readers."

Jason D. Otis
CEO of Catbird Printing
www.catbirdprinting.com

"Sometimes you have to go back to go forward, being physically repositioned to get in position for where you actually belong. Yohance has provided a practical solution for building and understanding communication skills that can bring about success."

Iesha O'Deneal
Senior Vice President,
Global Diversity &
Inclusion
Financial Services
Industry

"Communication is the key to success in every area of your life. Body language speaks louder than words, and can communicate your real feelings, no matter what your words say. This book teaches the tools to make sure you are "saying" the right things for your professional and personal life. Fantastic job!"

Eric Lewis
Commodity Trader

"At the beginning of the introduction, I knew this book was talking about me. I have had the same feelings of failure and helplessness. I did not know that body language that was outlined here had so much to do with success and communication. Then in the first chapter, he nailed me. Everyone wants to be liked. The techniques of body language and communication explained are straight forward and easy to understand. This is a book I am looking forward to reading again and again to practice and improve my self-confidence and change my outlook in life."

David Hyatt
Owner/Photographer
HyAtt Photography

"The Art of Communication presents the reader with easy to use body language techniques that can be used to improve their personal and professional interactions."

Clifford Lowdenback
DMD,MSD
Orthodontist
Lexington Kentucky

"Yohance does a fantastic job of describing the vital role that accurately reading body language played in his proactive approach to sales success. This important tool has enhanced his daily interactions at work, church, and with family and could most certainly aide everyone who puts it into use."

Trent Steele
Federal Agent

"In a fast paced world full of self indulgence and self concern, it's good to know that someone is listening and teaching others to do the same. This book can speak to us all. Everyone wants to be listened to and loved. *The Art of Communication* is easy to read, and understand."

Kris Perry
Professional Chef

"As an HR professional, I spend a good portion of my time on employee relations; coaching managers through difficult conversations with their employees. I always try to remind them that although there is work to be done, we are dealing with people. I can appreciate a resource like '*The Art of Communication*' because it reminds us that we all have a desire to be understood. Approaching any tough conversation with the goal of seeking to understand goes such a long way, so I loved the the techniques and reminders in the book, as well. Great read, overall."

Angela Webb
HR, Business Partner

"I REALLY enjoyed your book! Your own personal stories in your book truly will make the connection with everyone in some way, shape, or form. Having taught junior high and high school (mostly high school) for the past 10 years in a special education setting, with students who suffer from dyslexia, ADD, reading disabilities, and more, this book can open up their eyes to how to relate with the world with confidence."

Daun Edwards-Griffen
Speech Language
Pathologist

This book is the perfect choice for anyone who tries to communicate an idea (teachers, consultants, sales people, business owners and others) on a daily basis because to sell that idea we also have to sell ourselves as a trusted source of information."

Jessica Terry Bergman
Managing Partner
Trek Advancement

The Art of
Communication

Yohance Parker

The Art of Communication

ISBN-13: 978-1469916040
ISBN-10: 1469916045

Photography by: David Hyatt
www.davidhyattphoto.com

Graphics by: Tenesha Polk
Chrysalis Designs
Models: James Myers and Ernesto Andujar

Editor: Antoinique Bowman
Editor: Maisha Parker

DEDICATION

This book is dedicated to those who have always seen the best in me.

To Maria & William L. Parker Sr.
My mother and father, who provided the loving environment for me to be myself and grow to man that God wants me to be.

To Demetrius, William and Adrian Parker
My brothers, who fought for me, carried me and laughed with me even when my jokes weren't that funny.

To Lolita Cartwright, Fontessa Booker, and Stephanie Lewis
My sisters, in your own way all of you have been a second mother to me.

To Kris White
My Life Coach, you taught me that no matter what, I could add value to the world.

To Jordyn Parker
My daughter, you will never know what having you in my life has done to me and for me.

To Maisha Parker
My wife, you are the catalyst that inspires, motivates and encourages me even when no one else is around. Thank you for listening to me practice my speeches, editing my work and always telling me the truth even when it hurts. I am blessed to have you.

CONTENTS

INTRODUCTION

For to be free is not merely to cast off one's chains, but to live in a way that respects and enhances the freedom of others.

Nelson Mandela

I began learning about body language in 2001 during my career as a car salesman. It was my first sales job and I have to be honest, I was the worst! During the first few months I really didn't sell anything and I knew I was close to being "boxed." For those of you who don't know what it means to be boxed, it's when your assistant sales manager boxes up all of your possessions and walks you out of the door. In other words, you have been "fired!"

Because of my gifted ability to run people off the lot as fast as they drove on the lot, I believed that my own personal boxing experience was on its way; in addition, they moved my little cubicle in the back next to the bathroom. Moving me to the back was their opportunity for me to fall on my own sword and put me out of my misery. But I had a goal and that was to succeed! I had no clue how to reach that goal, but I knew if I could just learn how to be a successful car salesman, I could sell anything!

THE ART OF COMMUNICATION

My new location in the back turned out to be the best thing that could have happened to me, because a few doors down from me was the top salesman in the company and I could see him at work. He wasn't the best looking person and he didn't have super charisma, but he was the very best salesman. He closed more deals than people I had spoken with the entire time I had been a car salesman. After a few days of watching this I knew I needed his help. I walked into his cubicle, hoping for a miracle, and asked him what I could do to become a better salesman. He reached onto his desk and grabbed three books: *Selling 101* by Zig Ziglar, *Goals* by Brain Tracy, and *Body Language: How to Read Others Thoughts by Their Gestures* by Allen Pease .

In four days I read all three books, and that was a miracle! I have dyslexia, but In spite of my disability, I challenged myself because I had a desire to improve. The body language book really caught my attention, so I read it two more times, from cover to cover.

My confidence and sales instantly improved. Through the knowledge of body language, I was able to build instant rapport and have deeper and meaningful relationships with my customers, more meaningful than I could have ever imagined. With body language I was able to build the type of client relationships that involved trust, trusting me enough to tell their friends and family members about me. They even called me their "friend." So instead of having to wait for customers to drive up, customers were calling and scheduling appointments with me! Reading that one book on body language completely turned my career around as a car salesman. I was amazed!

Three months after reading my first book on body language, I read ten different books on the same topic and went from the very worst car salesman to one of the top, constantly competing for the top salesman position. My main competition was with my friend who gave me my very first book on body language-you know the salesman I was next to when I was moved to the back cubicle. At the end of the year, he won "Top Salesman" and I received "Rookie of the Year," which I was more than happy to receive.

I observed other car salesmen struggling with building rapport with customers and handling rejections. I was excited to teach anyone who would listen to all that I had learned about body language. This book is a result of my ten year journey of studying body language and communication. It takes a step back to the very beginning when I first discovered body language-from my rapid failure as a car salesman to being moved to the back cubicle and then receiving the Rookie of the Year award. I read and studied closely more the 100 body language books and took many courses from some of the top body language experts from around the world. These books and classes helped me develop a deeper insight as to how the mind and body work together.

When I first started reading books on the subject of body language, I must admit that I had no clue of the wide range of information I would discover. The first book I read was really simple and written in a way that a complete novice could read and understand. But the more I studied human behavior and neurology, which is the core of body language; I fell deeply in love with understanding how the mind and body work together.

As a body language expert, my business is to train people to understand what their body language is saying and to learn how to read other people's gestures, movements, and facial expressions. I train people to understand their own body language so that they give their best first impression for social and professional situations. In all industries everyone is looking to get the advantage and many times the staff struggles with establishing relationships with clients, communication skills, and improving sales.

A few years ago a company hired me to coach one

of their salesmen who was not doing well and was very close to being laid off. Immediately, I noticed that his body language was completely closed and every word that came out of his mouth was negative. Closed body language ranges from arms crossed, legs crossed (ankles and knees crossed), and looking down or away.

When we were sitting in the sales meeting, his manager asked what he was going to do to turn his numbers around and he shrugged his shoulders and said, "I don't know." His manager then asked where he was going to find new business and he dropped his head down low and said, "I don't know." I could relate to how he was feeling because I felt exactly the same way in the early stages of my career as car salesman.

As soon as the meeting was over the manager looked at me and said, "He is all yours!" I overheard one assistant manager whisper to another, "It will take a miracle to help him improve." After hearing that comment, I thought to myself, "I was that guy." Flashbacks played in my head and I could remember seeing my name on the bottom of the sales board with the lowest numbers. I heard other sales guys make negative statements about me. For example, someone said, "He is the worst" and others were laughing at me. I knew that if I could improve that anyone could and it was my mission to use what

I learned to help this salesman.

The first thing we did was leave the building and go to the gym for a twenty-five minute workout. I knew that I had to change his mental state by changing his physical state. Just like I was, he was depressed and one of the best ways to combat depression is exercise. According to Dr. Bart Bishop, exercise releases endorphins, which gets rid of the bad feelings and amps up the good feelings. In two days, I had him feeling super confident and in a little over a week, he went from being the worst salesman to competing with the other salesmen.

First he learned what his negative body language was saying to others. We discussed how his client's first impression of him did not come from what he said, but what his clients sub-consciously read through his negative body language. Consequently, his body language affected his number of sales. Secondly, he learned how to read other peoples' verbal and non-verbal buy clues.

Improving his ability to communicate with others, both his clients and his co-workers, helped him to establish authentic relationships by displaying confidence and building trust.

He also used the information on body language to help communicate in other aspects of his life. And when I returned three months later to speak to the entire sales force and the office staff, he was the top salesman at that company and a year later, I found out that he was engaged to be married, which he contributed to body language. He gained confidence, which helped him better communicate with women and make a great first impression.

My book isn't like any other body language book, because I didn't become a body language expert in the formal way. I fell into the information because I was desperate. I honestly just didn't want to lose my job. However, after learning about the subject, I began taking classes, training with experts, and attending body language seminars.

While taking classes and training with experts, lots of reading was involved and I have severe Attention Deficit Disorder (ADD) and Dyslexia, so for me to read a book from cover to cover was challenging. The book had to be written in a way where the author was not lecturing me, as it is done in academia. So when I decided to write this book, I wanted to integrate my life story and my formal training of body language, so that my readers would understand and be encouraged by my story. I wanted it to have formal body language techniques with an autobiography feel.

I have always enjoyed autobiographies. I remember

growing up hating reading, and my mother would become so angry at me because I would never do my required reading for school or my bible. By the time I was in the seventh grade I was on a third grade reading level. That was the year we found out that I had dyslexia and ADD. One of the doctors told my mother that they had found that some children who have similar struggles with reading as I did, really enjoyed autobiographies. So she purchased the autobiography of Mr. T from the *A Team* television program, and while reading It, I found out that he has dyslexia too. I read his book so many times that the pages came loose.

My story will tell how body language saved my job and how it has helped me transition from a failing car salesman to Director of Operations of a company. It changed my life!

CHAPTER ONE
EVERYONE DESIRES TO BE LIKED

To understand communication, you have to understand how we are as humans. We have a desire to be liked, understood, and heard. Once you have a full comprehension of this foundation, it will have a polarizing shift in the way you communicate with other people, and that shift should take place in you, non-verbally and verbally.

From a young age, we all have an inner desire to be liked, and for most of us that desire started as early as four or five years old when we walked into a pre-school classroom for the first time and we glanced around the classroom looking for someone to acknowledge us. As soon as someone smiled at us and asked us to sit by them, our entire attitude changed. It changed because we had a new friend, and a new bond developed. Because someone expressed interest in you, that scared, sad look on your face transformed into a huge smile.

We all desire to be liked no matter where you are from or what type of background you come from; there is a burning desire to be liked. But getting people to like us is more of an unconscious process than conscious. The people that we like or most like are those that we have more in common with. The old, famous cliché that *opposites attract* might sound fun, but at the end of the day, we like those who behave like us, those who speak like us, and when we look at them we see ourselves.

Having the knowledge that everyone desires to be liked has helped me in my personal and professional life. I was able to release the stress and anxiety I felt when interacting with new people. At first, I became anxious at the thought of meeting someone new and the possibility that they might not care for me. My stress and anxiety levels increased! However, when I understood that they were just as worried and nervous as I was, I was able to relax, smile, and feel free. I felt extremely confident.

When I read *Signals How to Use Body Language for Power, Success, and Love* by Allan Pease, I understood how I could use non-verbal and verbal communication to build rapport with people. After reading the book, I tried some of the new techniques to see if I could get people to like me. Whenever I read something, I would immediately practice it. For me, that was the best way of learning. So I ventured to a coffee shop to try an experiment. I knew that there would be many people coming in and out and I strategically sat at a table that was in line with the cash register where people were ordering their coffee and walking to their seat. I used a clip board to record data on what worked and what didn't work. I wanted to see if I could get people to instantly like me. The following are the techniques I used:

- Raised Eye Brows and Open Eyes: This shows openness and interests. When we are face to face with someone that we know or when we see someone that we find physically attractive, we open our eyes wider and our pupils become enlarged. (Roshan Cool)

- A Genuine Smile: This technique shows that you are friendly, happy and that you are interested in the person. When we smile genuinely our teeth show. (Russell and Fernandez-Dols)

- Power of our Touch: When we touch another person such as giving someone a hug, shaking someone's hand or giving someone a high five, science tells us that the touch triggers the release of our brains endorphins which helps us feel better and gives us energy. (Brooks S. Edwards, M.D. Mayo Clinic Staff).

- Pointing your body: When our shoulders, knees, and feet are pointed in the direction of the person that we are speaking with that tells them that we are interested in them and what they are saying. (Shelly Hagen)

My experiment started once the person got their coffee and sat down. I would raise my eye brows, open up my eyes, make confident eye contact, give a genuine smile, and say hello. I made sure that when I said hello that my shoulders were pointing in their direction, so each person knew that I was interested in what they had to say, that I liked what they had to say, and that I liked them. I made sure that I verbalized that I liked either something that they had on or something that they were saying. For example, one gentleman arrived in a very interesting outfit and it was easy to see that he was very uncomfortable in what he was wearing. He kept pulling at the bottom of his shirt and he was carrying his book bag pulled half way across his chest, almost as a shield. As he walked in my general direction, I made strong eye contact, smiled, and said, "Hello!" In a soft tone, he said, "hello." I immediately matched the soft tone and the pace of his voice. We enjoy hearing people who sound like we do. Matching the soft tone of his voice and the pace of his voice helped him feel more comfortable. I raised my hand with the palm up and shook his hand, synchronizing at the speed he was moving.

Instantly, his face went from being very tight and nervous to being relaxed and softened. We spoke on a number of different topics for thirty minutes. One of the employees mentioned that he had never seen that guy speak to anyone. Usually, he just sat in the same spot keeping to himself and reading the paper.

When I connected with him, a strong bond started to form between the two of us and a friendship evolved from it. By the end of our conversation he knew that I liked him.

<u>TECHNIQUES TO REMEMBER</u>

- Raised Eye Brows and Open Eyes: Shows openness and interest.

- A Genuine Smile: When we smile genuinely our teeth are showing.

- Open Body Language: Knees apart, legs stretched out, elbows away from body, hands not touching, legs and arms uncrossed.

- Power of Our Touch: Hug, handshake or hive five

CHAPTER TWO

EVERYONE DESIRES TO BE UNDERSTOOD

The deeper that we understand people the deeper we will connect with them.

Yohance Parker

As a parent of a three year old daughter, there is nothing more beautiful than to see her sitting down learning something for the first time. I remember when she first learned how to write the letter "H." Earlier that day her uncle taught her how to do it. When she arrived home later that afternoon she didn't do what she normally does, which is run and jump into my arms, she went into my office and grabbed a sheet of paper and grabbed one of her crayons and said with an extremely, exciting voice, "daddy look what I can do. " For the next two to three minutes she tried over and over to show me what she had just learned, but she just couldn't do it and I couldn't understand what she was trying to show me.

A lot like my three year old daughter, we really

desire to be understood. We might not start to cry and outwardly show our frustrations as my three year old daughter did, but inwardly we still show the same frustration, anger, and pain.

To show people that you understand what they are saying, here are some simple verbal and non-verbal techniques you can demonstrate:

Techniques You Can Demonstrate:

- Your body pointing in the direction of the person that is speaking. If your legs are crossed make sure that they are crossed towards the person who is speaking.

- Focus on the person speaking, ignoring any distractions. Avoid checking your cell phone, reading the menu, and try to give them your uninterrupted interest. Tune out the background.

- Gazing- shows that you are attentive to what the person is saying. The more that you are interested in something the less you blink.
  (David J. Lieberman)

- Make physical contact- when we are interested in someone, we make contact with them, this could be a high-five, a hug, or a solid hand shake.

- Find a quiet place if you are in a room full of people.

- Control your pace- Speak slowly, focusing on making sure that the person who is listening can clearly understand you.

When my daughter felt that I couldn't understand her, I knew I had to calm her down and help her relax so she could explain to me what she was attempting to show me. I looked directly into her eyes and said, "Jordyn daddy loves you" and I gave her a warm hug and a big high-five. I then told her to show me at the dining room table. I sat down right next to her and in a soft spoken voice told her to show daddy what she had learned. With a huge smile on her face she was able to show me that she had learn to write a capital "H." She jumped up and gave me a huge hug!

Knowing that people desire to be understood will help you establish strong relationships and build rapport with others. I was able to build a true bond with my daughter, because I put her needs first. Slowing down and taking the time to find out what others truly desire and not my own needs allowed me to read my daughter's non-verbal communication.

<u>TECHNIQUES TO REMEMBER</u>

Everyone Desires to be Understood
- Body pointing in the direction of the person that is speaking.

- Focus on the one speaking- you have to ignore any distractions.

- Gazing- shows that you are attentive to what the person is saying. The more that you are interested in something the less you blink.

- Make contact- when we are interested in someone make contact with them, could be a high-five or a hug or give a solid hand shake.

- Find a quit place

- Control your pace- Speak slowly, focus on making sure that the person who is listening can clearly understand you.

CHAPTER THREE

EVERYONE DESIRES TO BE HEARD

When we take the time to listen to someone we show that we care.

Yohance Parker

When I started working on this chapter I was sitting in a coffee shop with my laptop opened, and deeply engaged in writing in my next chapter.

While typing I noticed that there was a gentleman near me who was also typing on his laptop. As he was typing tears were rolling down his cheek. I walked over and grabbed a handful of napkins for him to wipe away the tears. As he was wiping the tears away, I asked if everything was okay and if there was anything that I could do to help him. He told me that a year ago his wife, while serving in Afghanistan, had been killed and he was writing a book about her, their marriage, and his healing process.

My first thought was, "What do I say to this man?" I didn't know him and I had never experienced such a tragic loss nor did I personally know anyone who had experienced this type of tragedy. Initially my inclination was just to ignore the situation altogether. I wanted to either continue working on the chapter of my book, go to another table or worst, leave.

Despite my hesitation, it was easy to see that he wanted to talk. I was sure that he could tell that I was bit uncomfortable and nervous about saying the wrong thing. I knew that if I was in his place I would want someone to listen; so despite my fears I decided not to run away, but to stay and be the best listener that I could be.

I saved the chapter that I was working on and closed my laptop. I turned my body so that my body was facing his. I made sure that my face was soft, (which means I wasn't tightening my face by biting down on my teeth or squinting my eyes. I have noticed that when I become really nervous or if I am focusing, I tighten my face, and some people feel that I look mean and a little intimidating). I told him that I was very sad to hear about the death of his wife and asked him to read me the chapter that he was working on.

I made sure to focus and to stay fully present in the moment, which was a little difficult with people walking around and other people having conversations all around us. The following are the techniques I used to help me focus and stay in the moment:

- I asked questions when I heard something that deeply interested me; this was also good to help me remember key points.

- I asked him to repeat himself when I did not clearly hear or understand something he said. This helped me to not lose my focus when the chapter seemed a little long.

- I held a pen between my index finger and my thumb in both my right and left hand. This helped me to not be so fidgety.

I was able to focus and stay in the moment for the entire chapter, which for someone who has attention deficit disorder was extremely hard. To communicate that I was listening to him, I used these non-verbal cues:

- I kept constant eye contact with him as he was speaking (Michael Ellisberg).

- The louder it got when other people were laughing or talking, I leaned in closer to him (Linda Lee)

- Every few minutes I would nod and smile and commented with words or phrases like, "very sweet or nice." (Shelly Hagen)

- At the halfway point of the chapter, I encouraged him to continue and told him that I would love to hear the rest of the chapter (David J Lieberman).

- When I had a question or wanted to make a point, I would place my left index finger on the outside of my lips and when he would look at me and pause, I would then speak (Allan Pease).

During the conversation with the nice gentleman, I might have said twenty-five to seventy-five words, but at end of our conversation he was deeply thankful. He continued to thank me for an entire minute.

As I was driving home and re-played that entire conversation, I realized that even though I had never experienced a loss of that kind, I was able to connect with him. Part of our connection was because we have had similar experiences, but showing him that I was a good listener made it easier to form a bond.

TECHNIQUES TO REMEMBER

Everyone Desires to be Heard

- Keep constant eye contact with the person as they are speaking (Michael Ellisberg).
- When people who are around you get louder, you should lean in closer to the person you are speaking with (Linda Lee).
- Every few minutes nod and smile and encourage the person with words of praise (Shelly Hagen).
- At the halfway point of the conversation, encourage the person to continue (David J. Lieberman).
- When you have a question or want to make a point, place your left index finger on the outside of your lips and when the person looks at you and pauses, you can then speak (Allan Pease).

CHAPTER FOUR
EVERY DAY APPLICATION

Each year the interest in body language increases and has become a very popular subject. Major local and national news channels have had body language experts on most or all of their shows, especially during the election season. During the 5:00, 6:00, or 10:00 o'clock local news and even CNN or MSNBC, you will witness a body language expert decoding the non-verbal language, revealing the inner thoughts of the candidates. Even more popular than the non-verbal expressions of the political candidates is the lives of celebrities. There is endless media coverage on who is in love with whom, who will stay together, or who might not be a true match for the other.

The first time I saw a body language expert on a news Show was when Michael Jackson married Lisa Marie Presley. On one channel the body language expert said, "Look how he is gazing into her eyes; it's definitely true love." On another channel a body language expert said, "Look at how they are not walking in sync, this relationship won't last."

I laughed so hard because in my mind I said there is no way that anyone could look at someone and tell if they will stay together, and look what happened, Michael and Lisa Marie separated and divorced. They may have been in love, but the marriage did not last. There was some truth to what their body language was saying. I should have paid more attention to those two body language experts.

I have been studying non-verbal and verbal communication for over ten years. Watching those two body language experts on television that day did not entice me study verbal and non-verbal communication, it was out of fear and desperation. I was an absolutely horrible car salesman who was on the fast track to being fired.

I remember my first day at the dealership like it was yesterday. When I walked into the dealership the general manager told me that the cubicle near the door was going to be mine and he said jokingly, "top producers sit closer to the door." I waited for my instructions. Finally, he told me to have a seat and the assistant manager would be in shortly to start my training session, teaching me all I needed to know to be successful. I watched him walk away and thought to myself, "he is a great leader and I wish he was training me." He was a man that displayed complete confidence, from his walk, to the way he spoke, and they way he carried himself.

When he spoke with me, I felt that he believed in me and my abilities to be successful salesman.

After sitting in my very empty cubicle for an hour, the assistant manager walked in with a huge smile on his face, hair slicked back, in an all black custom made suit, white shirt, and a black tie. He walked past my cubicle, gave me the "what's up" nod, and proceeded directly to the sales desk. He sat at the sales desk for another thirty minutes practically ignoring me while relaxing and drinking his coffee. Finally he walked over to me and said, "Follow me." By this point I was slightly irritated and confused. I began thinking that he was the worst leader that I had ever met. After sitting for thirty minutes and watching him walk past me repeatedly, ignoring me I felt like he didn't care who I was. I reluctantly followed him to the training room with very low expectations for what was in store for me. He grabbed a box of the product knowledge DVDs for all of the vehicles and put the first one in and told me to view each one. Relieved to have the chance to finally get some formal training I sat down and prepared to learn. During the video training, I took more notes than I had ever taken even in college. After watching all eight DVDs, I walked to the sales desk to inquire about the next step of my training. My charismatic assistant manager clapped his hands and said, "That's it; now it's time to get to work!" I thought to myself, "Oh my God, I'm in trouble!" I went back to my cubicle and watched the other salesmen; most were sitting in their cubicles just like I was, but there were one or two who were standing by the door waiting for potential customers. Others were standing outside smoking. I thought that it would be smarter to be outside, so I left my cubicle and stood outside so I could be the first one to speak with the customers that drove up.

I didn't take the first car that pulled up because I wanted to see how the salesmen with more experience handled it. I stood there and watched a few of the other guys approach customers and then I was ready. My first customers were a man and his wife standing by a row of cars. After spotting the pair I walked over to them briskly as if I was power walking. I walked faster with every step, and I'm sad to say that by the time I reached the couple I had sweat dripping down my head, the palms of my hands felt like a soaked wash rag, and my mouth was completely dry. When I said hello, my lips were dry and white as if I had kissed a chalk board. As I approached the couple, I said hello, trying to be as polite and energetic as possible. When I reached out to shake the nice gentleman's hand, I was so nervous that I did what is called the Bone-Crusher (Allan Pease). The Bone-Crusher is an aggressive handshake with extreme force. When someone uses that type of handshake, they are extremely aggressive or nervous. Many times when people use the Bone-Crusher, they are trying to hide their nervousness by over doing the hand shake and saying, "look how strong and confident I am." But the truth is they are just the opposite, weak and insecure, just like I was. My first customer could feel my insecurity.

A similar hand shake is the Vise; that's where the palm of the hand is positioned downward, which is a dominate position. As the person is shaking the other person's hand, they apply extreme force and aggressively shake the other person's hand.

Both the Vise and Bone-Crusher are extremely, aggressive handshakes and will instantly turn the one who is receiving it off. These handshakes do not encourage friendliness (being open) or sincerity, and will not help build instant relationships with customer. Most of the times it will have the opposite effect, and they will become instantly closed towards you and not interested in what you have to offer.

Their response was closed body language and within fifteen seconds of our handshake, he and his wife ended the conversation and told me that they were looking for a another vehicle. They quickly returned to their car and sped down the highway. But the story doesn't end there. That following Saturday, they returned to the dealership and purchased the same vehicle with another salesman. That was painful and didn't help my insecurity.

Since I had no clue how to build rapport with customers, the next few days and weeks did not improve. When new customers drove into the dealership, in the initial thirty seconds of meeting them, I did such a poor job that they instantly return to their current vehicle without even test driving a vehicle. This is known as "burning" a customer. Burning customers is when you approach a new customer so badly that they leave within five minutes of arriving.

A little over a month had passed and things had not gotten any better. The general manager was very concerned and called me into his office. Imagine how it felt to be called into the office by the general manager, especially when you knew that you were not doing a good job. It was not a good feeling! He reminded me of the first time we met during the interview and how he was instantly drawn to me; he felt that I had great promise, and could be one of the best car salesmen. Those words, "the best car salesman" rang a bell and I immediately thought of the mutual friend that referred me. He also believed that I could be one of the best car salesmen that they had ever seen. It was very hard to believe that because, I hadn't sold one vehicle. I was living off my draw, which was financially challenging. The draw is small amount of money you earn for your work, like an hourly wage. As your sales increase, you are paid by your monthly sales commission and you no longer receive the draw. The draw is not a great living and dealerships make sure you know that!

Since he believed in me and knew that I could improve, my general manager asked me what he could do to help me. I desperately told him that I needed training. He encouraged me to spend time with the assistant manager, who had a wealth of knowledge and he knew I could really learn from him. I was so thankful that he didn't fire me, so I quickly ran to my assistant manager and asked for help. Given that I had no clue how to sell, I appreciated any tips or training he would offer me. I was so excited as we walked back to the training room and I just knew he was going to teach me how to be a car salesman, but he pulled out those product knowledge videos and I instantly stopped him! I told him that I had already watched those videos a number of times. I didn't need more product knowledge. What I really needed and wanted was people knowledge! It was my desire to know what to say to the customers and how to say it. I needed a mentor, someone I could shadow and watch demonstrate how it is done. He smiled at me and told me to meet the customers on the lot, invite them to come inside, and he would talk to them and teach me how it is done.

THE ART OF COMMUNICATION

With a new zeal for car sales, I went back to standing outside by the smokers and waited for the next car to pull up. I walked right over to a lady who had pulled onto the lot to look at one of our shiny, new cars and I approached her, saying hello and immediately asked her to come to my office so that she could meet my assistant manager. She looked at me as if I had asked for her purse and all of her money and she instantly said, "No thank you," turned around, and walked to her car. A few hours later, I noticed that the same lady returned to the dealership, but she was not alone. She was with a man who could have been a boyfriend or her husband and they were talking to another car salesman. I felt like a horrible car salesman and by the numbers on our sales board, I was horrible. Again, I was moved to another cubicle. They moved me far in the back next to the men's rest room (which was a sad metaphor to say that you stink). I just knew my days were numbered.

The challenges I was facing as a struggling car salesman caused me to reflect on the time when I first was diagnosed with *Dyslexia and Attention Deficit Disorder*. I sat back and thought about being tested in the seventh grade for dyslexia. A few days after the test, I was separated from the other students and moved to a special education class.

Immediately, I felt like I was a failure, but I reminded myself of all that I went through while in special education classes and knew that I was going to make it. My mother was my cheerleader and she supported me through these circumstances, and researched different means to help me through this ordeal. She found an autobiography of a famous person who had ADD. That person was Mr. T. He wrote about how he was able to be successful despite being diagnosed with Attention Deficit Disorder.

Remembering that, on my lunch break I went to the library and looked up every famous person who had dyslexia and attention deficit disorder. I wrote all of their names down and the different learning techniques that some of them used. I then went back to my little cubicle and wrote their names down everywhere I could find an empty space. I decided to use one of the techniques that I read about. I proceeded to take a highlighter and highlight all of my books and all of the paper work that had to be signed by my clients. Highlighting the parts that I had to read helped me to process what I was reading.

From open to close I sat in my little cubicle and had no desire to talk to customers. I was quickly losing confidence in myself and my ability to do the job. I would read the newspaper's employment section, looking to see what job I could find once I was fired from the current one. I had never quit a job, but from the way things were going I wouldn't have to. Everyone knew that the writing was on the wall. Sitting just a couple of cubicles from me was the top salesman at the dealership; however, he was not in the back because of his lack of success, but because of his success. They needed to convert two cubicles to one large cubicle because of the amount of trophies and awards he earned for being the top salesman, month after month and year after year. The one month that he finished second was on his two month vacation. The first month of his vacation, he still received salesman of the month because he had so many customers that came in to purchase vehicles. The second month that he was gone he finished second by one vehicle. When he returned, he was upset that he finished second and not first and because of that, he didn't receive the bonus for being the number one salesman at the dealership. What was that "thing" he had, that even when he was on vacation his sales were at the top of the chart!

I watched him like a hawk hoping to see the secret to his unbelievable success. I diligently searched and I couldn't find anything. He was about 5'4" in height and he was balding with about five or six hairs at the top of his head that he would brush back. On one occasion he told me to answer his phone while he left to get a haircut and I thought to myself, "What hair was he going to cut?" However, I did stay and answer his phone. I wasn't doing anything else but waiting to get fired.

While sitting in his cubicle, I noticed boxes of books under his desk. I was very curious, so I rummaged through them and noticed that there were all types of sales books. When he returned from his quick haircut, I asked him if he would help me to improve my sales techniques, because at that time I didn't deserve to call myself a car salesman. He reached under his desk and grabbed three books. Honestly, I was immediately disappointed because I was hoping he would enlighten me and tell me all of his secrets on how to be a great car salesman, but he just handed me three books: Zig Ziglar's *Sales 101*, Brian Tracy's *Goals, and Body Language* by Allan Pease. As I was walking out of his cubicle, I thought maybe he was testing me like a young Jedi knight. These three books would normally take me a long time to read, maybe a day and a half. I was instantly intrigued by the information I read in the body language book. The very next day I went to the library to search for more books on body language. I really wanted to understand this concept.

After reading Allan Pease's book and other books on body language, I became a body language junkie. I took out as many books as the librarian would allow me to checkout at one time. I was blessed that they had old cassette tapes because I only had an old cassette player. I listened to one of the tapes so much that it ended up breaking and they made me pay $11.00 for it. I thought to myself that it was worth it because I had pages and pages of notes from the one tape.

I remember reading how President John F. Kennedy (JFK) commissioned and completed a study on the most effective handshakes and how you could understand a person's intentions by understanding their handshake. During his presidency, he was able to discern the type of leaders and people he encountered by their handshake. Through a soft handshake, he was able to recognize if a person was secure or if they struggled with insecurity and if that person was quick to let go, he   knew that person was arrogant John F. Kennedy Commission on handshake. When a person pulls the other person closer when shaking hands, it shows controlling body language. A hand that is pushed away at the end of hand shake means that the person has a negative feeling towards you. (Linda Lee)

President Kennedy's own handshake made a strong statement and a good first impression. Leaders of different countries recognized that he was a strong, decisive leader that was trustworthy and secure of the decisions he made as President of the United States of America.

When I found out how important JFK felt about shaking hands, I realized that learning how to shake a customer's hand could possibly help me as a struggling car salesman and would be the first step in building relationships with my customers.

From that study, I quickly learned why my first customer was completely turned off by my first impression. I lacked the knowledge to build instant relationships and show trust. That customer was very interested in purchasing a vehicle and he did that day, but not from me. He also returned to the dealership a few weeks later and purchased another vehicle for his wife, but I was not the salesman. I have spent the last several years studying the art of handshakes and I have learned that a person can create a positive environment if they understood how to effectively shake hands.

TYPES OF HANDSHAKES THAT I USE

The handshake that I use the most is called the "upper hand." Because this is a submissive handshake, I apply 1% less pressure than what the other person is applying. The "upper hand" instantly allows the person I have made contact with to feel relaxed and to know that they do not have to put up a shield. This handshake shows that I am secure in who I am and what I am saying. My goal is to make the person that I am speaking with feel comfortable and relaxed and when people are comfortable and relaxed, they are more open and happier and willing to listen to new and different ideas without feeling defensive. (Allan Pease)

(Upper Hand)

The *"First Impression"* Process Using the Upper Hand Handshake

As a car salesman, I have noticed that most people who decide to visit a dealership are guarded because of the three following reasons:1) fear of being taken advantage of, 2) afraid they will not receive a fair deal for their trade, and 3) worried about a high interest rate. To help them bring their guard down, I would calmly walk towards the car of the potential customer, making sure that I allowed them time to get out of their vehicle. Next, I walked over to the vehicle they were interested in, paying attention to the pace in which the customer walked toward the vehicle, because that is the pace that I would walk over. Once I was five to ten feet from the customer, in a pleasant tone, I would greet them and thank them for deciding to spend time at our dealership. I would stand outside of their personal territory (I will talk about personal territory in a later chapter.) and slowly extend the upper hand. I looked directly into the customer's eyes, smiled, and raised my eye brows. If the wife walks over as I am shaking hands with the husband, I would keep eye contact with the first person (husband) for one second and then instantly make eye contact with the wife. I made sure that the customer was the first person to let go of my hand, because I wanted the customer to feel in complete control. I turned my shoulders, hips, and feet in the direction of the wife or the other person. If the wife took the time to walk over to be a part of the first impression process, I instantly knew that she was either the main decision maker or held a lot of weight in making the decision. By giving both people the upper hand and equal time of acknowledgment, it allowed both customers to understand that I was giving them all power in the situation, and that they were the main focus.

If I am negotiating with someone or competing with someone I will offer them the "vertical" handshake. The vertical handshake shows that we have mutual respect for one another and that we are both equal. I apply the same amount of pressure that I am receiving.

(Vertical Handshake)

One of my favorites' is the "hand hug" handshake. This is when you shake hands vertically and then you place your left hand onto the other person's right hand. With this handshake, you are perceived as being friendly, kind, warm, and welcoming. I only use this handshake with people that I have already established a relationship with. As you have built rapport with people and they have allowed you into their space, the "hand hug" handshake moves from the left hand on the person's right hand, to placing your left hand on their elbow, then bicep, and lastly, shoulder. I only use the extended version of this handshake with men and older women. This is a more intimate handshake.

(Hand Hug)

OTHER TYPES OF HANDSHAKES THAT PEOPLE USE

The "Dominate" handshake is used when a person wants to take control and dominate the other person. When using this handshake, the person's palm is down and the other person's palm is up. A woman might use this if she desires to show authority or leadership in a situation where she is in a position held predominately by men.

(Dominate Handshake)

CLOSED BODY LANGUAGE

When I gave any customer the upper hand, which is the palm of my hand facing up, their body language instantly changed from becoming closed to open and receptive. A few ways that a customer demonstrates closed body language:

- Their arms are crossed
- When giving the upper hand, they slowly uncross their arms to shake to reciprocate the "upper hand." It is important to always allow them to release the hand shake so that they have a clear understanding that they have the power, not you.
- Tension in their shoulders and jaw line
- Hands behind their back or deep in their pockets
- You approach the customer with a smile, but they do not smile back, and they look down away.

(Closed Body Language)

When I smiled, raised my eye brows (we will talk about how to use your smile, eyes, and raised eye brows in later chapters) and offered them the upper hand, I did not immediately talk about what vehicle they might be interested in; but instead, I would tell a joke or something funny about myself to help them relax. I did not bring up the topic of the vehicle until they did, even if it took an hour or two. Humor and laughter are great ways to open someone's body language. One way to use humor is through the concept of self-deprecation; this is when you use humor to make fun of yourself. Self-deprecation is a great way to build rapport with someone who is closed. It allows them to see you as an equal and most importantly, to see you as being open and honest. Another way to open closed body language is the "high-five" gesture. For those of you who are not familiar with the "high-five," it is when one person holds their hand up in the air and the other raises their hand to make contact with the other hand. Both palms touch flatly in the middle. I am a person who loves "high-fives." It must be from my athletic days in high school and college. When a person would have their arms crossed or body turned away from me, I would always find a way to give them a high-five and 99% of the time the person would instantly smile and open up their body language. I would normally ask them about their favorite sport teams or what school they attended and this would bring on a high-five moment.

(High Five)

When the customer has signed the paperwork and is about to take ownership of their new vehicle, I always gave them the "double-hander." This is a very popular handshake for people in the corporate environment. This handshake conveys to the customer "I truly appreciate your time and your business." As I gave the double-hander, I would graciously smile, slowly lowering my head in a slow bowing motion as a gesture of humility. My desire is for the customer to feel like a champion and when the customer feels like they have won the battle, especially in the area of car buying, they feel victorious!

When I did not use the "double-hander" after the customers signed the documentation, I noticed that my customer service scores were usually in the middle range and rarely did my customers send me business from their friends and family. But as soon as I implemented the double-hander, my customer service scores were excellent and instantly customers expressed their intent to refer friends and family to me. One comment from a customer was, "I have finally found an honest car salesman." After hearing that statement, I was so encouraged that I almost jumped for joy! One of the hardest things for me with regards to selling cars is people's perception and negative opinion of car salesmen, and personally that bothered me. Most car salesmen in the industry desire to assist the customer with having a wonderful car purchasing experience.

Another type of handshake is the "two-handed" handshake, which shows sincerity, authenticity, trustworthiness, and an intimate connection. Other two-handed handshakes are the wrist hold and the elbow grasp. There is also the upper-arm grip, which is between the elbow and the shoulder blade and then the shoulder hold. The two-handed handshake allows for a person to have more physical contact, a deeper connection, and it allows you to be in the other person's personal space. However, you have to be careful when using the two-handed handshake, because if your relationship isn't as deep as you think, the other person will feel very uncomfortable.

My transition from an unsuccessful car salesman to a successful car salesman seems to happen overnight. Integrating the information I learned from body language was a vast part of my overnight success. Instantly, I began building great rapport with customers, all due to the simple ability to shake someone's hand and make them feel welcomed, like a close friend or family member. The feeling was awesome!

With my new body language information, I was constantly finishing among the top salesmen at the dealership. Witnessing my success, some of the other car salesmen asked me daily how I turned my sales around. I was extremely eager to share my story and I started coaching those who were interested in the art of body language and how to use it to better communicate. The General Manager had a proposition for me. He asked if I would train the new guys, and as soon as he asked, I thought about the assistant manager and how he trained me by playing those product DVDs. Replaying that scenario in my mind brought back memories and I instantly said, "Yes!" I was excited about training the new salesmen.

At this point early in my career, I felt like the sky was the limit. I began reading books on non-verbal and verbal communication; in addition, I enrolled in a body language certification course. The course taught the basics behind reading body language, and how to identify and describe language that displays different emotions. As I sat in my cubicle reading, my general manager walked towards me and told me to walk the lot with him. Walking the lot meant that a car salesman would walk around the entire dealership to see what inventory was on the ground. While we were walking, he gave me a compliment and told me that when he sees me, he sees more than just a car salesman and that I should consider what I want to do with my life. I told him about my desire to become a motivational speaker and he thought I would be great at that. Those were very encouraging statements and gave me an extra boost of self-confidence. The next day my general manager didn't show up for work. I was told he had retired from the auto industry, which really sadden me, because when I was struggling, he supported me. He was my boss and my coach.

A few days after my general manager left, I had the opportunity to really put the body language techniques to a true test. It was an extremely slow Tuesday, which was very common. A co-worker and I watched a large pick-up truck pull into the dealership. On his license plate were the words, "I support my flag" and right under that statement was a rebel flag. My co-worker looked at me and said, "He's all yours" and quickly fled to the parts department. My first thought was "I'm sure that he would rather speak with someone who was white and not a black male," but right then I knew this was the perfect opportunity to see if body language really, truly works. It was time to put the theory to the test!

He quickly jumped out of his truck and began looking at the pre-owned trucks that were on sale. As I stepped out of the door, I was going over what my body language needed to say in order to create a positive environment for us to have positive dialogue. I immediately told myself that I needed to show confidence and professionalism.

Naturally, my first thoughts were, "this guy is going to hate me and not want to speak with me and most likely he will want to speak with someone else." I felt my body wanting to be closed. At one point, as I was walking towards him, I wanted to put my hands in my pocket. In the past, putting my hands in my pocket was something I did when I became nervous. I could even feel my face starting to frown and my shoulders starting to come closer and hunch over. I was withdrawing, almost like going into a shell. Putting my hands in my pocket and bringing my shoulders forward meant I was trying to make myself as small as possible, which many of us do when we are scared. Our sub-conscious tells us that we need to make our self small and hide. When we show a lack of confidence with our body language, people feel that we are lying or not telling the entire truth and they will be slow and quite apprehensive to build a relationship with you.

(Open Body Language)

Confident body language involves correct posture. It is shown when your shoulders are back, you're standing tall, and your back is not bent over. In addition, you shouldn't have your hands in your pockets or behind your back. Your hands should be in plain sight, so people can see that you have nothing to hide. There is no frown on your face, but you are smiling, not only with your mouth, but also with your eyes. Smiling with your eyes is when your smile pushes up into your eyes. Research says that this is the sincerest smile. (Daniel Nettle) When you are confident, you hold your head high and make great eye contact, not being afraid to look people directly in their eyes while you're speaking with them. People trust those who are confident and they desire to be around them, building relationships. I knew that if I showed a lack of confidence in my body language, this guy would know it immediately and would not respect me or do business with me.

THE ART OF COMMUNICATION

I took long strides as I was walking towards him. I was encouraging myself by repeating, "This guy is going to like me and I will show confidence." As I approached the customer, I greeted him with a warm smile and said hello. At the same time, I slowly raised my hand giving him a vertical handshake, because my desire was for him to understand that we are equals. He took a second and then shook my hand. As we shook hands, I rotated his hand up to give him the upper hand and as soon as I gave him the upper hand, I noticed that his shoulders slowly lowered and his face softened; however, he still asked if there was someone else who could help him? I looked directly in the eyes and told him that I was one of the senior salesmen here and would be the one who would assist him. After that I just stood there and didn't say anything else. I could feel my shoulders wanting to hunch over and all of my fingers tingling, wanting to hide inside my pockets. All of my studying on body language said that confident people were open, so I was trying to be super open and I continued to look directly at him. After what seemed to be a lifetime, he started to ask me about our selection of trucks.

The end result was I sold him a beautiful pre-own truck. But it didn't stop there; he referred his wife to me and she bought a car and then he recommended his best friend and within two weeks, he purchased a new truck. I'm not sure if our encounter changed his opinion about black people, but I do know that body language was a powerful tool in that situation and my desire, then and now, is to learn as much about body language as I can.

TECHNIQUES TO REMEMBER

Every Day Application
- Upper Handshake: Allows the person that you are shaking hands with to know that you are open and honest, have nothing to hide and you are there to serve them.

- Open Body Language: Communicates acceptance, vulnerability, honesty, and that you are not concealing anything.

- Eye Contact: Shows that you are confident, that you are paying attention, that you are interested, and a good listener.

- Vertical Handshake: Shows that we have mutual respect for one another and that we are both equal.

- Hand Hug: Shows that you are warm, friendly, trustworthy, and honest.

CHAPTER FIVE

INTERVIEWING

Working at the dealership was extremely fun, but at the same time was very emotional, mentally, and physically draining. I was working thirteen to fourteen hour days. Financially I was making more money than I ever dreamed about, but moving further away from my dream as a professional speaker.

In the car business, you meet so many interesting people and I had an opportunity to meet the Vice President of Marketing of a national mortgage firm. Our relationship began when I sold him a vehicle and from that sale, he thought that I would really enjoy working in the mortgage refinance industry. He said that the hours were better and I would not have to pound the pavement in the hot Texas 100 degree weather. The thought of getting out of the hot Texas sun put a huge smile on my face and gave me the push I needed to try something different. My success in auto sales empowered me, and I felt that I could be an instant success in the mortgage refinance industry. I was excited to see how body language would help me soar to be among the *top* in a new industry.

After calling the Vice President of Marketing, he gave me the telephone number of the Regional Director who had an immediate need for a loan officer. I remember thinking that if he hires me, he would send me to the worst team so that I could make them the number one team! Yes, I was young, arrogant, and not too smart, but I kept thinking that if I could be successful in selling cars, I would be successful in the mortgage refinance business. It was going to be the easiest job I've had since working at Dairy Queen for two weeks when I was fifteen years old.

I had two days before my interview with the Regional Director and I spent those two days reading and practicing body language that would help me be at my best during my interview. The books that I read to prepare were *How to Say It at Work* by Jack Griffin and *Definitive Book of Body Language* by Allan Pease.

TECHNIQUES THAT I WAS FOCUSED ON USING:
Be Relaxed
- o Minimal movement with arms and legs.
- o Keep feet flat underneath you.
- o Chest should be completely open.
- o Arms, knees and ankles remain relaxed

to avoid stiffness.
- While listening make sure that your mouth is closed and head nodding while listening.

Appear Confident
- Make eye contact while listening and speaking.
- Walk with a fast pace, to show that you are energetic.
- Hold your head vertically and make sure that your shoulders, knees and feet are pointing to the direction of the person speaking with you.
- Speak loud and clear; synchronize your voice to their pace of speaking and their volume.
- Make sure that you have proper posture.

Make A Confident Entrance
- Acknowledge the receptionist and those who are in the lobby area.
- Walk with a purpose, don't hesitate.
- Smile as soon as the receptionist looks at you.
- Have your hands by your side and as you're walking make sure that you don't walk with your hands in your pocket.

THE ART OF COMMUNICATION

I woke up early the morning of my interview and went to the gym to work out so that I could feel my best and look my best for my interview. I arrived thirty minutes early wearing my favorite black suit. As I sat in the lobby, I made sure that my body language expressed someone who was confident and a professional.

TECHNIQUES I USED TO SHOW CONFIDENCE

- I sat in a chair that had back support and not the long, soft couch

- While sitting, my back was straight and not hunched over

- As people walked by me, I would clearly say hello in a confident, loud tone, making sure that I could be heard and understood.

As the Regional Director walked towards me, I looked directly in his eyes, showing confidence in my eyes. I made sure that I was the first one to raise my hand (in the upper hand position) to show that I was a leader, a decision maker, and not someone who was passive. I had a warm and charming smile, and stood as tall as I could with my back straight and shoulders back. As we walked into his office I chose the chair on my left side, which was his right side. As a sign of respect, I waited to make sure that he sat down first and then I sat down. I learned this from the book *Body Language How to Read Other's Thoughts* by Allan Pease. By allowing him to sit first, I made a non-verbal statement that said, "I respect you, your environment, and your leadership." Such respect is shown in the presence of the President of United States or the Queen of England.

He spent a few seconds reviewing my resume and then he looked up at me and asked about my sales experience. I again made strong eye contact and paraphrased the question he asked me, matching the same pace that he was speaking and his tone of voice. I told him about my experience in the auto industry and how I started off as the worst car salesman and ended my career as the second top salesman, receiving numerous awards including Rookie of the Year.

Whenever he would ask questions I made sure that I leaned forward, just a little to show that I was listening and I raised my eyebrows to show that I liked his questions and that I was interested. During the interview I made sure that the palms of my hands were visible, so that he knew I was being open and honest.

In the beginning of the interview, which lasted three hours, he asked a number of easy questions, but towards the end, the questions became more difficult and I could feel my body language closing.

He created a scenario in which I had no experience and asked me how I would handle it. Again, I could feel my entire body closing, but I knew if my body was closed, I would not be at my best. On the other hand, if my mind and body were open, then I would be free to new possibilities and innovative ideas. I took a deep breath and focused on having open body language and answering his questions to the best of my ability. Once I was finished answering his questions, he leaned back in his chair, folded his hands behind his head, and he asked me, "are you sure that you have never worked in the mortgage field?" As soon as he leaned back in his chair, I knew that I had the job. His body was no longer tight, but now relaxed. I also noticed that his breathing was slow and steady, and the pace of his speaking was also slower. His shoulders were no longer leaning forward but his shoulders were now leaning back.

He looked at me and smiled and said that normally the interviewing process involved two to three different interviews, but he felt that I was the one they were seeking to make a difference in the company. The interview was on a Thursday, and I started working the following Monday.

<u>TECHNIQUES TO REMEMBER</u>

Interviewing

- Sit in a chair that has back support and not the long, soft couch
- While sitting, keep your back straight and not hunched over
- As people walked by, clearly say hello in a confident, loud tone, making sure that you can be heard and understood.
- Strong eye contact-shows confident and trust.
- Synchronize your speed and the pace of your voice.

CHAPTER SIX

VERBAL FOUNDATION

I had started my new job as a mortgage loan office. Unlike the car dealership, this company had the greatest training that I had ever experienced. The training that the company provided was focused on both product knowledge and personal development. Before we were even able to talk with the client we went through five weeks of training. At other companies you were very fortunate if you received five days of training. The instructor was awesome and the information was priceless, but as I sat there and listened to the information, I heard something that was never discussed in the interview. All communication that I would conduct with the customers would be done completely over the telephone

What was I going to do? I have been studying body language, and in my mind, all of my success came from learning to present myself in a way that the customer could physically see me in person and know that I was open, honest, and available. I was in trouble!

After a full day of learning about the mortgage industry, I went home feeling extremely humbled and worn out. As soon I rested and had a long jog, I started reading a number of my favorite body language books, studying how to use pauses and voice tone in daily conversations. Nicholas Boothman's book *How to Make People Like You in 90 Seconds or Less* helped me understand how to use non-verbal communication in my daily life.

In his book he referred to the Neuro-Linguistic Programming approach or (NLP). This really caught my attention. **Neuro-Linguistic Programming consists of three elements:**

- Neuro is derived from the Greek word "neuron" for nerve

- Linguistic is derived from the Latin word "linga" which means language

- Programming refers to the process of arranging the collection of systems.
  (Shlomo Vaknin)

Neuro-linguistic programming was founded by Richard Bandler and John Grinder. Wikipedia explains NLP as an approach to explaining human behavior, thought, and communication. NLP describes how people represent and communicate with the world and provides principles or techniques for identifying thought patterns and behavior.

NLP was amazing for me and just like when I first started learning about body language, I purchased every book that I could find on NLP; I started taking NLP classes to gain a deeper understanding and to learn how to communicate successfully using NLP communication styles.

In the NLP approach, there are three foundational components of verbal communication:
- Rapport
    - Relationship, connection, especially harmonious or sympathetic.

- Calibration
    - Calibration is the art of taking a "mental snapshot" of a person's emotional state(s)

- Communication Styles
    - Visual
    - Auditory
    - Kinesthetic

Using these foundations, I was able to develop the skills that were needed for me to be successful in verbal communication. What surprised me was how the non-verbal and verbal work hand in hand. I first thought that they were separate, but I quickly found out that you cannot be successful with one if you are not focused on the other. I immediately thought how much more successful I would have been in the auto industry if I would have learned the NLP communication styles before.

NEURO LINGUISTIC PROGRAMMING

Review

- Neuro-linguistic programming-an approach to explaining human behavior, thought and communication.

- Neuro is derived from the Greek word "neuron" for nerve.

- Linguistic is derived from the Latin word "linga" which means language.

- Programming refers to the process of arranging the collection of systems.

- Neuro-linguistic programming was founded by Richard Bandler and John Grinder.

- The foundation of NLP verbal communication is Rapport, Calibration, and Communication Styles.

CHAPTER SEVEN
VERBAL BONDING

BUILDING VERBAL RAPPORT

Building rapport using body language was relatively simple when I understood the foundation of everyone desires to be liked, heard, and understood, but with this new job, I had to translate that into verbalization. I knew that I needed to do more than just tell people that I liked them, heard them, and understood them.

When I started working in the mortgage refinance business, I knew that even though the customer couldn't see me, my body language had to be completely open, because our mind and body are congruent with one another and work together. If my body language was open, then my mind would be open. The opposite is also true. If my mind was closed then my body language would also be closed.

THE ART OF COMMUNICATION

FACIAL EXPRESSIONS

I made sure that I had a comfortable chair, but that the chair would allow me to sit up straight. I always kept my palms up; my arms never crossed and my feet and legs never crossed. The most important piece of equipment that I had in my cubicle was a mirror. I would glance at that mirror before every phone call and make sure that before every phone call my eyes were wide open, my eye brows were as high as they could be lifted, and that I had a smile on my face.

Even when I wasn't sure of the answer to a question I made sure that my facial expressions were still open. I noticed that whenever I was nervous or didn't know the answer to a question, my facial expressions would instantly start to become closed. My eyebrows would become lowered and my pupils would become smaller. I even noticed wrinkles around my eyes, mouth, and forehead area. The more closed my facial expression became, the angrier and older I looked, but when the conversation with customer was successful, my facial expressions were soft and I looked younger, happier, and excited.

VERBAL SYNCHRONIZATION

As to be expected, on the first day of training I was

extremely nervous and excited. I had to concentrate on learning new information regarding all of the laws and rules for mortgages and my new verbal techniques. My first call came through and it was a nice lady from New York City. The first few verbal techniques I focused on were the speed of her speech and the volume of her voice. She spoke really fast and very loud. I matched her speed and volume, meaning I spoke fast and loud. When verbally synchronizing yourself with someone else, you're validating that person's self concept of how they sound, and they are hearing something very familiar.

To help build stronger rapport, it was important to find common ground, so I didn't begin the conversation talking about refinancing her mortgage. While matching her speed and volume, I told her my mother was from New York and that I still have family there. She commented that she knew that I was from New York and I laughed and told her that I was from Kentucky, and that I had been there only to visit my family. After we confirmed that we had common ground, I started talking about how I could help her refinance her mortgage. She had spoken with three other companies, but she felt comfortable with me.

I wish that I could say that I was super successful immediately, but that was far from being true. I was struggling, floating in the middle of the pack. I knew that I needed to practice verbally synchronizing my speech patterns a lot more than just at work. It needed to be second nature. It didn't matter if I was at the grocery store or the mall; I worked on verbal and non-verbal synchronization. As an exercise, I watched television for an hour and for the first thirty minutes; I watched the program with the picture and sound. For the second half of the show I would cover the television screen so that I was not able to see the actors. I listened for a few minutes and then I would choose one of the actors to synchronize my voice with. The most difficult character on television for me to synchronize with was the character Kramer from the television show *Seinfeld*. Because of his gestures and sounds he made, it was difficult for me.

After a few days of practicing, I was able to synchronize verbally with almost anyone. In order to build common ground I would match the tone of their voice, the speed at which they spoke, the volume of their voice, their trigger words (which are words they use frequently), the number of pauses used in their sentences, their speed of breathing, and their voice inflections.

<u>TECHNIQUES TO REMEMBER</u>

- Number of pauses used in their sentences
- Their voice inflections (Statements, Commands, Questions)
- Trigger words
- Tone of voice
- Speed at which they talk
- Volume of voice
- Speed of their breathing

CHAPTER EIGHT
VERBAL MIND READING

Calibration is the art of taking a "mental snapshot" of a person's emotional state(s).
Keith Livingston

How do you use body language techniques when there is not a body to analyze, only a voice over the telephone? I could not examine or study a handshake, tell if their body was closed, or read what their eyes were saying. All I had was a voice, and the only thing I could do was listen. How was I going to build rapport with my customers and get them to trust me-over the telephone? That was my dilemma! To solve this problem, I had to apply a technique that would help me understand, through their voice, how they felt emotionally and mentally. I learned to look, listen, and feel for clues and cues as my customers responded to our conversation. Calibration was a great tool to utilize and it was a powerful tool for me. In Neuro-Linguistic Programming (NLP) "calibration" refers to using our sensory acuity (sharpness) to gauge the mental and emotional state or mood of a person or audience.

THE ART OF COMMUNICATION

According to Michael Hall Ph. D, calibration sharpens with experience, and is a critical factor in the success of any NLP intervention, because when delivering a pattern, TIMING IS EVERYTHING.

While working in the mortgage refinance industry, I learned that communication is important, especially when you are dealing with people and their finances. There is a certain way to communicate with them and I had to be extremely sensitive to their emotional and mental state.

In the beginning of every phone call, it was important to verbally synchronize my speech pattern to match the customer's speech pattern; in doing so, I was able to build rapport and find common ground. Once I established a strong connection, I guided the conversation to the topic at hand, which was helping them improve their financial situation.

I always began the conversation with a customer on a positive and upbeat note. Immediately, I would focus on the mental and emotional state of the person. This allowed me to gauge the customer's pattern. I gauged the customer's pattern by asking questions and finding common ground. Once our connection was established, I would always guide the conversation to their financial situation.

VERBAL CUES I USED TO GAUGE THEIR RESPONSE:
- How do you feel about...?
- What do you think about...?
- Have you?
- Do you?
- Did you?

The customer's verbal responses allowed me to know their mental and emotional state before the customer could ever reject my proposal.

CUES THAT SUGGEST AN EMOTIONAL OR MENTAL CHANGE:
- Well
- Hmm
- Yeah
- I'm not sure
- Well maybe
- If only
- Um
- Err
- Ah

If I noticed any anxiety I would explain the benefits a little deeper while keeping a positive upbeat and reassuring tone. I would also synchronize the pace and tone of my voice and I matched my breathing with theirs. These techniques allowed me to re-establish rapport with the customer while addressing negative response.

POSITIVE RESPONSE CUES ARE ALWAYS EASIER TO IDENTIFY:

- The pace of their speaking is faster
- They laugh
- The pitch of their voice is higher
- Their pronunciation of words has power and sparkle

Before I learned how to apply calibration, I was stuck using only the sales and product scripts that were provided, and because of that, I missed some sales opportunities in the early part of my mortgage career. I failed to notice the small, simple, unconscious clues that calibration taught me. By noticing my customer's small emotional changes (stuttering, worrying, being nervous, heavy breathing, and dry mouth), I was able to address their concerns. Most people, when dealing with important decisions, experience those emotional changes. Understanding calibration techniques can help you take the appropriate steps to refocus your client and give them a sense of peace.

HOW BECOMING A VERBAL MIND READER HELPED ME TO BE SUCCESSFUL

- I was able to realize when a client was not satisfied with my proposal before they verbalized it. This was great because I never saw the client in person and could not read their negative body language. By listening to their verbal emotional responses I was able to redirect my approach and address their unconscious rejection.

- I knew what was mentally and emotionally important to my clients and was able to use this to build a stronger level of rapport or establish rapport.

- I was able redirect their focus from a negative, mental, emotional direction to a more positive direction, helping them to synch their attitude with mine.

EXAMPLE OF HOW BEING A VERBAL MIND READER WAS USEFUL FOR ME

I went over a proposal with a female client and I felt that I had established a foundation of strong rapport. Both of our voices were very positive and upbeat. Her situation was not extremely difficult so I really didn't have to sell her on refinancing. I knew that she had spoken to anther mortgage company before me, but she let me know that I did a better job following up with my proposal and that I was more professional.

It was time to close the deal and I noticed that she sighed softly and then asked me to hold on while she got a drink of water. That was the first time she mentioned needing a drink of water and hearing her softly sigh suggested to me that her emotional state had changed. I instantly stopped with the proposal and asked her how long she had lived in her home. After she answered telling me that she had lived there for over forty years and that all five of her sons grew up in that house. I noticed that she sighed again. At that moment, I realized that I was no longer in control of the direction of our conversation.

The pace of her speaking had become very slow and the tone of her voice was deeper. I needed to find out what the setback was and how to get her back to a positive state. I ask her, "you really love this house?" and she answered with a "yes I surely do!" She said that with a positive bounce in voice. As I spoke with her, I reminded myself not to start my sentences with *don't, do not, haven't or have not or any word with no or not in it*. I wanted to make sure that both of us were using positive words as often as possible. I did not recall having such a hard time with a proposal or closing a deal since I learned calibration. Before learning calibration, I would start most of my sentences with negative words, almost eighty percent of the time they never agreed to close with me.

After she answered "yes I surely do!" with a positive bounce in her voice, I immediately asked her to tell me the most beautiful memory she had with her

Chapter Eight

family in that home. She told me of how her husband (who was deceased) and her son's would play tag football outside after watching football on Saturday and she would sit on her porch and watch them. She said that her older son had been helping her ever since her husband had passed away. I then asked her if she didn't mind if I went over the information with her son. Automatically she said "yes!" almost yelling her response to me. I immediately noticed a huge change in her voice. She spoke faster and louder and even seemed to be smiling. I then asked her to do me a favor, and I could hear her sitting up in her chair ready to hear my request. She had changed physically and verbally. I told her that I just emailed her an authorization letter allowing me to speak with her son about her personal information. She then went on to tell me how helpful her sons were and how they were all married, except the youngest one. She didn't think he would ever get married. The conversation was completely joyful. I told her that I was going to go to lunch and that she could fax it to me the next day. By the time I returned from lunch she had already faxed the authorization letter back to me.

I called to thank her for her returning it so quickly and before I could tell her that I would call her son when he got off of work, she was already calling him on three-way. I reviewed the information with her son and he agreed that it would work for his mother. Shortly after we ended the conversation with her son and without any further hesitation she signed with us.

When communicating on the telephone or in-person, calibration is an effective tool, and allows thorough investigation of a person's emotional and mental changes. It is a technique where true trustworthiness and rapport is established.

TECHNIQUES TO REMEMBER

Signs of Mental or Emotional Changes

- The changing of breathing patterns
- Speaking pace becomes slower (Ian R. McLeren)
- Hesitation (Stephen Juan Ph. D)
- Stuttering (Stephen Juan Ph. D)
- Pronunciation becomes more drawn out (Ian R. McLeren)
- Voice pitch changes (Peggy Noonan)
- Notice the change in tone (Peggy Noonan)
- Be aware of sighing (Ian R. McLeren)

CHAPTER NINE
STYLES OF COMMUNICATION

What kind of communicator are you? Do you create visual images in your mind when others are speaking? Are you able to discern the meaning of someone's words by listening to their verbal expressions? Or when you are speaking, do you need to have something in your hand? These three questions reveal three styles of communicators: visual, auditory, and kinesthetic.

Before learning about visual, auditory, and kinesthetic styles of communication, I thought everyone communicated in the same way. I did observe that my connection was deeper with some people but I thought that was because we had things in common such as similar sports, friends or music.

I had just passed my ninety day probation and finally became one of the top ten mortgage loan officers, but I knew that I had the ability to do even better. I began studying and reading more books on verbal communication. I read the following books: *Words that Change Minds* by Shelle Rose Charvet, *Persuasion Engineering* by Richard Bandler & John La Valle, and *Unleashing Your Brilliance* by Brian E. Walsh. After reading those books, I learned that we all have different ways of communicating, and understanding each other's communication styles will allow us to build stronger relationships and have a deeper understanding of people. For example, in Charvet's book, I was able to understand how our language and behavior will first influence ourselves and then those around us.

Studying the different styles of communication was the major turning point in my career and I was able to understand how people communicate; in addition, I could communicate with them in a way that they could better understand me.

The way that we communicate is an unconscious cognitive process. When someone is speaking with us, we don't think about how we are receiving the information, we just receive it and before we blink an eyelash, we respond to the question or statement without putting much thought into it. In this same way, we unconsciously either connect with the communication style of the person or we miss that really small space that keeps us from fully connecting. I am not saying that you cannot establish rapport with them, but you will struggle with fully connecting.

In the following pages, I will explore each communication style to help you recognize your own communication style. I will explain how understanding the different styles have helped me to be successful in the mortgage industry. That success led to recruiters from all across the country calling me to work for their company. Having recruiters interested in me was very encouraging, because I had only been in the mortgage industry for six months.

TECHNNQUES TO REMEMBER

Three Types of Communicators

- Visual Communicators
- Auditory Communicators
- Kinesthetic Communicators

CHAPTER TEN
COMMUNICATION ASSESSMENT

When I first started studying styles and types of communication, there was an abundance of information available. I found some very interesting information, but not very useful. I needed information that would help me to understand how people communicate and how I could establish instant and meaningful rapport.

I remember in college learning about the passive, aggressive, passive-aggressive and the assertive communication styles. The passive communicator was someone who avoids expressing their thoughts feeling and opinions. The aggressive communicator is someone who will stick up for themselves, and can be quick to become verbally abusive. The passive-aggressive communicator is someone who will indirectly express their frustrations. The assertive communicator is someone who is expressive at expressing their thoughts and feelings.

This information would have been great if I was dealing with relationships, but I needed to understand and learn how to simply speak with people.

Neuro Linguistic Programming (NLP) communication styles worked best for me; I was able to immediately apply it to my personal and professional life. The three styles I focused on were: kinesthetic, visual, and auditory.

We all use these three communication styles in our everyday use of words but there is a primary style that we all have, and in this assessment you will be able to find your primary communication style.

1.   When you are trying a new recipe for the first time you
   V.   Read and follow a recipe step by step
   A.   Ask someone to help you
   K.   Use your gut feeling

2.   When you are lost do you
   V.   Immediately use your map for directions.
   A.   Stop to ask for directions
   K.   Use your gut feelings

3.   When following instructions do you prefer to
   V.   Read the instructions
   A.   Listen to someone explain how to do it
   K.   Learn by trial and error

4.   Your first memory is what
   - **V.**   Visualizing it
   - **A.**   Being spoken to
   - **K.**   Doing it

5.   When you are anxious you
   - **V.**   Visualize the worst-case scenarios
   - **A.**   Talk the situation over in your head
   - **K.**   Have a hard time keeping still, constantly fiddle with things

6.   When you have a complaint you would rather discuss it.
   - **V.**   In Writing
   - **A.**   On the phone
   - **K.**   In Person

7.   When listening to music you
   - **V.**   Read the lyrics while listening to the music
   - **A.**   Sing along with the music either to yourself or aloud
   - **K.**   Your body automatically moves to the beat of the music

8.   Your main interests are
   - **V.**   Photography, watching movies or people
   - **A.**   Listening to music, talk radio, books on CD, talking with friends or family

K. Doing physical activities

9. When you teach someone something you
    V. Write the instructions
    A. Verbalize your instructions
    K. Show by actions

10. Phrases that you tend to use
    V. Can you paint me a picture
    A. Do you hear what I am saying
    K. I know how you feel

11. You feel especially connected to people because of.
    V. How they look
    A. Your conversation you had with them
    K. How you felt after meeting them

12. Most of your free time you enjoy
    V. Watching movies or television
    A. Talking with family and friends
    K. Doing physical activities or making things

13. When studying for a test you
    V. Read over your notes and use various colors
    A. Are comfortable working with a study group or reading your notes aloud
    K. Physically working your formula out

14.   You remember best by
       V.   Taking notes
       A.   Hearing information and repeating it
                 out loud or to yourself
       K.   Doing and practicing in the activity

15.   When you first contact someone on the
       phone you
       V.   Arrange to meet face to face
       A.   Are comfortable talking to them on the
                 phone
       K.   Feel uncomfortable

16.   You first notice how people
       V.   Look and dress
       A.   How they speak
       K.   How they walk and stand

17.   Activities that you might enjoy
       V.   Visiting museums or galleries
       A.   Listening to music or having great
                 conversations with family and friends
       K.   Physical activities or creating things

18.   When meeting with a friend you might say
  V. It's great to see you
  A. It's great to hear from you
  K. You give them a hug or shake their hand

19.   You find it easiest to remember
  V. Faces
  A. Names
  K. Things

20.   You think that you can tell if someone is lying because
  V. They avoid eye contact
  A. Their voice changes
  K. You have a negative vibe about them

Communication Assessment Score Sheet

Mark an X in the box for each question. For example if your answer for question one is V then you would mark an X in that column. When you have completed the assessment you will add up the columns and total each column at the bottom. The column with the highest number would describe your individual communication style.

Communication Assessment Score Sheet

QUESTION	V	A	K
1			
2			
3			
4			
5			
6			
7			
8			
9			
10			
11			
12			
13			
14			
15			
16			
17			
18			
19			
20			
TOTAL			

CHAPTER ELEVEN
VISUAL COMMUNICATORS

If you are visual communicator, then you and I communicate in the same way. We speak in terms of how things look or we create visual pictures in our minds as someone is describing an event. In a discussion, visual style communicators try to get people to see their point.

Visual style communicators enjoy being noticed. They wear clothes that are colorful and fashionable. Hairstyle, makeup, and accessories are important to them and they like to catch the eye of other people. When describing experiences they use words like clear, dull, colorful, and bright. (Sally Dimmick)

VISUAL COMMUNICATORS LIKE
- Written instructions
- Enjoy observing and watching.
- Memorize best by seeing words or images on paper.
- Being on time
- The "Big Picture"
- Visual aids and power point presentations

VISUAL COMMUNICATORS DISLIKE
- Verbal instructions
- Noise easily distracts them.
- Are easily bored if there is no direction or plans.
- Too Many details
- If people or projects are late

VISUAL COMMUNICATOR ADVANTAGES
- Able to recall things that they have read.
- Great at the transitioning from one subject to another smoothly and quickly.
- Proficient time managers.
- Terrific at coming up with "big picture" ideas.
- Able to create long term vision.
- Quick to learn difficult concepts.
- Able to look and see that something is out of alignment, or not horizontal or vertical.

VISUAL COMMUNICATOR DISADVANTAGES
- Struggle with explaining how they came to a conclusion or have a hard time communicating their thoughts.
- Difficulty "unlearning" incorrect information.
- Not flexible when faced with timing or changes.
- Have a hard time focusing on details.
- Constantly rushing others and themselves.

Visual communicators many times have strong opinions on how things should look and if they have a strong personality or are in a leadership position, it could sound as if they are saying this is how things should be.

Visual communicators can sometimes be critical of others due to the way they communicate, seeing other people's deficiency and imperfections. Great careers for visual communicators are sales or advertising, film, television, graphic design, computer animation, artist and architect.

When I first started working in the mortgage industry, I could see why I was able to build immediate rapport with specific people quicker and easier than others. My conversations with people who were also visual would flow more naturally. I would paint a picture for the customer, helping them to visualize how I could help them improve their financial situation. I would use the phrase "can you see what I am saying" and they would respond that they could clearly see what I was saying.

It is important that you are able to notice commonly used phrases that visual communicators use. When you hear someone use these common phrases you can build immediate rapport with them, because they will feel as if you understand. The most common statement I heard people say about me was "unlike other sales people, I could see their needs.

COMMON PHRASES VISUAL COMMUNICATORS WILL USE:

- Let's look at this differently.
- See if you understand this.
- I get the picture.
- I see what you mean.
- I can't quite picture it.
- I would like to get a different perspective.
- This is making me see spots.
- Can you see the big picture?
- Please clarify what you are trying to say.
- I can now see what you are where talking about.
- I never forget a face.
- Let me draw you a picture so you will understand what I am trying to say.
- I can visualize what you are telling me.
- That makes me see red.
- Please draw me a diagram so I may better understand what you are saying.
- Don't keep me in the dark
- I just don't see it
- That's not clear enough
- Get a mental picture
- You can plainly see
- Appears to me
- You are a sight for sore eyes

BUILDING RAPPORT WITH VISUAL COMMUNICATORS

While working in the mortgage industry, there were a number of tools I used to build solid rapport with visual communicators. I designed a visual communication guideline and list of advantages. I followed these guidelines as I spoke with my visual customers, and I continue to utilize them in all aspects of my daily activities.

- At the beginning of each meeting I would clearly go over the agenda for that meeting; let the visual client know the approximate length of time the meeting will last; and give them the agenda for the next meeting.

- Emailed or mailed highlighted notes of the information that will be covered in the meeting.

- Keep meetings short.

- Make sure that the customer is in a quiet environment with not many distractions.

- Be direct and to the point.

- If I changed my meeting agenda, postponed or rescheduled a meeting, I made sure that enough time was given in advance.

I noticed that by using my visual communication guidelines, I was able to build instant rapport with clients over the telephone and many times after the initial conversation, they would decide to commit to my company.

My interaction with visual communicators was completely structured around their strengths. Most of my phone conversations were short, direct, and to the point. The clients would compliment me on how organized I was, and how they felt well informed.

I found that the most effective way to maintain strong rapport and loyalty throughout was to email highlighted notes of our conversation, and send an email reminder of our next meeting, along with a copy of the agenda.

One of my most successful deals was with a lady who I instantly realized was a visual communicator. In the beginning of our conversation, she informed me that she could see the entire process going a certain way. As soon as she said that I said to her, "allow me to paint you a picture of what the steps of your entire process would look like." After going over the agenda of our next meeting she asked if I would send a note of all the documentation that she would need to finalize the deal. Not only did I know that we had great rapport, but I also knew that she was satisfied with choosing me and the organization I worked for.

BREAKING RAPPORT WITH VISUAL COMMUNICATOR

- Sending long emails

- Bombarding with too many details

- Communicating appointment changes at the last minute

- Taking a long time to get to the point

WORDS THAT VISUAL COMMUNICATORS USE:
- Analyze
- Appear
- Bright
- Clarity
- Clear cut
- Clearly
- Conspicuous
- Distinguish
- Dull
- Enlighten
- Envision
- Clarity

THE ART OF COMMUNICATION

- Focus
- Foggy
- Hazy
- Horizon
- Idea
- illusion
- Illustrate
- Imagine
- Inspect
- Look
- Notice
- Observe
- Obvious
- Outlook
- Perception
- Picture
- Pinpoint
- Scan
- Scene
- Scope
- Scrutinize
- See
- Show
- Sight
- Sketchy
- Spot
- Survey
- Vague
- View
- Visualize

TECHNIQUES TO REMEMBER

Building Rapport with Visual Communicators

- Keep meetings short

- Communicate the established start and end times.

- Be direct and to the point

- Communicate schedule changes well in advance

- Make sure that the client is in a quiet environment with few distractions.

- Email highlighted notes

CHAPTER TWELVE
KINESTHETIC COMMUNICATORS

While working in the mortgage industry, kinesthetic communicators were my favorite clients. They communicate their feelings. Once I noticed that the client was a kinesthetic communicator, I knew my job was to help them be as passionate as I was about the services my company could provide for them. I knew that they based their decisions on how they felt about me and my company.

During my conversations with kinesthetic communicators, their first words were, "hold just one moment; let me get a piece of paper and a pen to take notes." That was my first indication that I was speaking with someone who was a kinesthetic communicator.

KINESTHETIC COMMUNICATORS LIKE
- Details
- An organized agenda
- Expressing their thoughts and feelings
- Clear concise points
- To feel good about things

KINESTHETIC COMMUNICATORS DISLIKE

- Conflict
- Being rushed
- Being interrupted
- To many choices

KINESTHETIC COMMUNICATOR ADVANTAGES

- Loyal
- Team Players
- Detail Oriented

KINESTHETIC COMMUNICATOR DISADVANTAGES

- May complete tasks slowly
- Indecisive
- Avoid conflict
- Easily overwhelmed when presented with too much information

BUILDING RAPPORT WITH KINESTHETIC COMMUNICATORS

One of the most common communication traits that I noticed with those who were kinesthetic communicators was they spoke a little slower than I did. I had to immediately synchronize my body movements and the pace of my speaking which helped me build rapport with kinesthetic communicators.

Kinesthetic communicators focused on their sensation of how something feels to them, and how someone's words have touched them. To build strong rapport with a kinesthetic communicator, you need to appeal to their strong emotions. You want to appeal to their emotions because they base their decisions on how they feel about something. It's important to build on their emotions. You should use a combination of sound and sight to create sensations of being touched emotionally and physically. (Terry Mahoney)

A soft touch or a tender word is a great way to show that you are interested, listening, and that you care. Some kinesthetic communicators can be difficult to motivate until you are able to make them feel what you are talking about, but once you have motivated a kinesthetic communicator, they will be your number one supporter.

I was having a conversation with a lady who owned an animal shelter and wanted to refinance her mortgage but wasn't sure if she should choose my company or another one. She informed me that the other company's rate was a little better, but their customer service skills were not up to par. She didn't feel a connection, like she felt with my company.

Instead of going over the benefits of what my company could offer her, I went over a list of ways that she could help more dogs at the shelter by improving her financial situation. For the rest of our conversation, I didn't even mention her loan but, we talked about her dogs-which she felt a stronger, emotional connection with. At the end of the conversation she told me without me mentioning anything that she had decided to go with my company. My client told a number of her friends about me and the services I provided.

How to Verbally Build Rapport with Kinesthetic Communicators

- Create a comfortable environment by having a prepared agenda.

- Communicate the established start and end times.

- Give a large, specific number of choices.

- Make sure that the client is in a comfortable chair and room with good lighting.

- Provide small amounts of information.

- Show that you care about their thoughts and feelings.

- Address how the client feels mentally and emotionally.

BREAKING RAPPORT VERBALLY WITH KINESTHETIC COMMUNICATORS

- Not allowing time for the client to make their decision.

- No prepared agenda.

- Overwhelming the client with a large amount of information.

- Interrupting the client while they are communicating their feelings.

- Being very confrontational.

QUESTIONS TO HELP YOU IDENTIFY A KINESTHETIC COMMUNICATOR:

- Why do you feel this way about the decision?
- How do you feel about what was said?
- Can you feel what I am saying?
- Does that song move you?
- Do you have a sense of what you are going to do?
- How does this feel for you?
- How did that movie touch you?

- Do you feel that you have made the right choice?

While working with kinesthetic communicators, I had to make sure that I was patient, very organized, and agenda focused. While explaining new information I had to be sure that the client was able to understand all of the new information and I had to be patient and sensitive in my response to their questions.

I always asked if they felt that the information was easy to understand and if they had any questions I would slowly explain each important detail. After the meeting, I would I immediately email them the information, so that they could go over their concerns and feel more comfortable.

WORDS AND PHRASES THAT KINESTHETIC COMMUNICATORS USE:

- Active
- Bearable
- Charge
- Let us touch upon this
- Affected
- Hope that you are comfortable
- I need you to walk me through this
- Callous

- I am very excite that you called
- Concrete
- Going with your company feels right to me.
- Emotional
- Let's catch up.
- I get the point that you are trying to make.
- What you said rubbed me the wrong way.
- Feel
- Firm
- It feels right to me.
- Not sure why, but that doesn't sit well with me.
- This fits.
- Flow
- Foundation
- Please help me to get a grasp on what you are telling me.
- Grasp
- Grip
- Hanging
- Hassle
- Heated
- Hold
- Hunch
- Hustle
- Intuition
- Lukewarm
- Motion
- Panicky
- Pressure

- Rush
- Sensitive
- Set
- Shallow
- Shift
- Softly
- Solid
- Sore
- Stir
- Stress
- Soft
- Stumble
- Support
- Tension
- Tied
- Touch
- Together
- Unsettled
- Whipped

TECHNIQUES TO REMEMBER

Building Rapport with Kinesthetic Communicators

- Create a comfortable environment by having a prepared agenda.

- Communicate the established start and end times.

- Give a large, specific number of choices.

- Make sure that the client is in a comfortable chair and room with good lighting.

- Provide small amounts of information.

- Show that you care about their thoughts and feelings.

- Address how the client feels mentally and emotionally.

CHAPTER THIRTEEN
AUDITORY COMMUNICATORS

Auditory communicators receive and communicate information using their sense of hearing, and can skillfully discern the true meaning of someone's words by listening to their verbal expressions. They are also very talkative and will vocalize what they think sounds best.

When I was working in the mortgage industry, it was easy to identify auditory communicators because they frequently used phrases like, "glad that you called and that sounds really good." Auditory communicators are very in tune to the sound of other people's voices. Because of my Kentucky accent, I was repeatedly asked, "where are you from"? The auditory communicator could immediately pick up the difference between the Kentucky accent and the Texas accent. Auditory communicators often remember exactly what they hear. I had to take notes because customers who were auditory communicators expected me to deliver everything that was promised.

AUDITORY COMMUNICATORS LIKE

- Remember names quickly.
- Enjoy acting in plays and movies.
- Would rather read out loud and not to themselves.
- Enjoy speaking in front of the class.
- Love music.
- Enjoys oral reports.
- Learns foreign languages easily.
- Learns best by listening and taking notes.
- Pick up new ideas and concepts quickly.

AUDITORY COMMUNICATORS DISLIKE:

- Reading silently for long periods of time.
- Written directions.
- Sharing conversation with others.
- People finishing their sentences.

AUDITORY COMMUNICATOR ADVANTAGES
- Follows verbal directions well.
- Able to pick out sound effects in movies.
- Great at explaining difficult information.

AUDITORY COMMUNICATOR DISADVANTAGES
- Hard to keep silent for long periods of time.
- Read slowly.
- Can be blunt or harsh

BUILDING RAPPORT WITH AUDITORY COMMUNICATORS

As soon as I noticed the client's communication style, I would synchronize my communication style with theirs, allowing me to build rapport and establish a strong foundation of trust. However, if I didn't use the same style, it would break rapport with the client. Instead of asking, "Do you feel that this loan would help your situation?" You would ask, "How does this loan sound to you?" Keep in mind that auditory communicators use their sense of hearing to communicate.

Ways to build rapport with auditory communicators:

- Empower the client.
  - Auditory communicators enjoy hearing themselves, so I would ask questions about themselves.
    Examples
    1. How does this sound to you?
    2. May we discuss what you mentioned earlier?

  - Ask questions that are connected to their strengths.
    Examples
    1. How often do you listen to...?

2. What did you say?

- Direct the conversation.
  - o Words you can use:
    1. Follow me.
    2. Let me direct you.

  - o Make sure the client isn't controlling the conversation.

- Recite Main Points.
  - o Quotes, dates, lists, and names.

- Focus on the Ending.
  - o When the client finished a statement, I would normally let the client know that I heard what they said. There are various ways to accomplish this:
    1. Repeat to them what they stated.
    2. Go over main points.

- Synchronization
  - o Synchronizing tone of voice, speed of speech, and volume.

- Change the speed of your speech
  - o People enjoy talking to people who speak the same speed as they speak

- Change the volume of how loud or soft that you are speaking
  - Auditory communicators are like speech volume that is be either as loud or as soft as their own

BREAKING RAPPORT WITH AUDITORY COMMUNICATORS

I wish that I could say that I always had excellent rapport with every client, but that's far from the truth. I noticed that when I spoke with clients who talked very fast, it would take me a few minutes before I was able to synchronize with them. On a few occasions, I synchronized with their tone of voice, speed of speech, and used visual words thinking they were visual communicators and five minutes into the conversation the client was doing everything that they could do to get off of the phone with me.

There were times when clients were only price checking and not truly interested in my company's services. When that occurred, I purposely broke rapport by either speaking faster than the client or speaking much slower than the client. I would also use the opposite words and phrases of their communication style; for example If the person was an auditory communicator, I would ask them if they could feel what I am saying or if they were a kinesthetic communicator I would ask them *if that sounds good to them?*

Ways to break rapport with auditory communicators:

- Changing subjects while the other person is speaking.
    - Takes the focus off of what the person desires to express.

- Constantly interrupting the person while they are talking
    - Understand that everyone wants to be heard and by constantly interrupting, it will immediately stop the flow of thought and speech

- Leave on hold for a long period of time
    - They will feel that you do not value their time

- Using non-auditory words and phrases such as feel, touch, grasp

- Turning on the television or radio during the conversation

- Texting or answering a phone call while the person is speaking

AUDITORY COMMUNICATION QUESTIONS AND PHRASES

I learned to really pay close attention to my client's words, phrases, and questions. This allowed me to understand their individual communication style. It was always easy for me recognize a visual communicator because we share the same communication.

With the auditory communicator, I focused on making the client feel that they had complete control of the situation. I would ask a short question in the area of their needs, concerns, and desires and let the client flow with the conversation.

QUESTIONS AND PHRASES AUDITORY COMMUNICATORS USE:

- That sounds about right to me.
- Could you explain that again please?
- I'm glad that you called.
- How does this sound?
- It's coming through loud and clear.
- I will talk to you later.
- What's your idea?
- Call me later.
- Chat soon.
- So good to hear from you.
- Tune in to what I'm saying.

- Sound good?
- Clear as a bell
- Talk with you later.
- Does this resonate with you?
- That's music to my ears.
- How can this be improved?
- Come again.
- Hear me out-Listen to what I'm saying
- I didn't hear that clearly
- We need to talk
- I can tell by your tone

WORDS THAT AUDITORY COMMUNICATORS USE:

- Announce
- Articulate
- Audible
- Boisterous
- Communicate
- Converse
- Discuss
- Dissonant
- Divulge
- Earshot
- Enunciate
- Gossip
- Hear
- Hush
- Listen

- Loud
- Mention
- Noise
- Proclaim
- Pronounce
- Remark
- Report
- Ring
- Roar
- Rumor
- Say
- Screech
- Shrill
- Shout
- Speak
- Speechless
- Squeal
- State
- Talk
- Tell
- Tone
- Utter
- Voice

TECHNIQUES TO REMEMBER

When Building Rapport With Auditory Communicators You Should:

- Empower the client
  - Auditory communicators enjoy hearing themselves, so ask questions about them
  - Ask questions that are connected to their strengths.

- Direct the conversation
  - Make sure the client isn't controlling the conversation

- Recite Main Points
  - Quotes, dates, lists, and names

- Focus on the Ending
  - When the client finishes a statement, let him know that you hear what they are saying or that it sounds perfect to you

- Synchronization
  - Synchronizing tone of voice, speed of speech and volume

CHAPTER FOURTEEN

ALL FOR ONE AND ONE FOR ALL

MARKETING FROM THE INSIDE OUT

After working in the mortgage industry for a number of years, a close friend of mine told me that I should think about the health care industry. She felt that I would find it extremely rewarding, fun, and super interesting.

After a few years of being in the health care industry, I found myself working as a Sales and Marketing Director for a Skilled Nursing and Rehabilitation center. The center was a small, older building that the local community saw as a "dump." This building inherited this reputation, not because of the staff's performance, but because it was one of the older buildings in the area. Getting referrals were very difficult and referral sources only send tough cases to dump facilities. Also, when they could not send patients to newer and nicer facilities, they would send them to the "dump."

Working in a building that was viewed as a dump had a negative impact on the staff. Whenever we had visitors, the staff's body language was closed; no one acknowledged the visitors by saying hello or asking how they were doing today. Due to the negative impact, the staff lacked the professionalism needed to create a positive and upbeat environment. I knew that if I was going to help improve the reputation of the facility, first I needed to help boost morale and motivate the staff.

I decided that I would equally divide my focus, devoting fifty percent to building rapport with my co-workers and motivating them to be excited about working in my facility and the other fifty percent was focused on marketing to current and new clients. This philosophy was different from other healthcare marketers, who focused all of their attention on building relationships with decision makers in the community.

MOTIVATING THE STAFF

While brainstorming about the best ways to boost staff morale, I instantly thought about my college soccer coach and how he would give us speeches before the game and at half time. Before the game started he would tell us that the game was more mental than it was physical, and no matter what the other team's record was, if we played as a team we could be the best! In his half time speech, he would tell us that we needed to stay focused and that we needed to encourage one another.

THE IMPORTANCE OF HUMAN TOUCH

I focused on creating a strong bond with everyone who I worked with. Understanding how to build instant rapport and how to engage and interact with others through human touch helped me to get my team excited, motivated, and ready to improve the reputation of our facility. Utilizing the power of physical contact allowed me to help people smile when they were not smiling; it also created an instant bond.

When I initially accepted the position as Sales and Marketing Director one of the first things I noticed was the huge gap, the size of the Grand Canyon, between the department heads and the rest of the staff. Department heads are those who hold a management position at the skilled nursing and rehabilitation facility. The department heads did not associate with the other employees on a personal level. The conversation between them was very task oriented and problem focused. There was very little staff appreciation or praise given by the management team. To close that gap between the leaders and those whose were not in a leadership position I used several techniques incorporating touch: (Allen Pease)

TECHNIQUES TO BUILD RAPPORT AND FRIENDSHIPS USING PHYSICAL TOUCH:

- High Five
- Fist Pound
- Pat on the Back
- Hand Hung

(Fist Pound)

Knowing when to engage is as important as the act of a positive touch, I always made sure that the other person made good eye contact and I intentionally made sure that there weren't any objects between myself and the other person.

If the person avoided eye contact or placed objects between us I would only give a pleasant "Hello." I was also aware of the cultural differences, being careful to always remain respectful. If their culture was to not make physical contact with a man other than their husband, then I would make sure not to give them a high five or any other physical contact.

Understanding the importance of what we say and how we communicate what we say allows us to have the ability to create a positive environment. For example, I have always used adjectives to help motivate myself and others around me.

ADJECTIVES THAT I USED TO HELP ENCOURAGE MY FELLOW CO-WORKERS:

- Awesome
- Great
- Excited
- Amazing
- Excitement
- Happy
- Phenomenal
- Exceptional
- Fantastic
- Magnificent
- Wonderful
- Brilliant
- Better than ever
- Marvelous
- Terrific
- Superb

- Fabulous
- Excellent
- Phenomenal

The more positive and upbeat my verbal and non-verbal communication was the more supportive and united the staff felt. My work relationships grew stronger and I started to notice the staff starting to work with me to improve the reputation of the facility from the inside out.

The first few months I made sure that I stopped by the facility before I made any sales visits. I walked around the facility so that I could intentionally say hello to every staff member. I would say, "Hello how are you?" to anyone that I made eye contact with. If anyone said "I'm ok" I would always stop and ask them if there was anything that I could do to help make their day go from ok to GREAT! My taking the time to speak with them made a major difference in their day. It changed their day just knowing that someone truly cared about their feelings.

Whenever someone asked how I was doing I would always use a positive adjective. Using positive adjectives gave the staff a sense of excitement, and saying those adjectives helped me feel excited about being at work.

GIVING OTHERS THE CREDIT

My number one goal was to be the internal cheerleader. I knew that I would have to motivate, encourage and help everyone to become excited about the new changes and growth that was going to come. I would immediately communicate any positive outcomes to the staff so we could celebrate as a team. By sharing the credit of my successes, I was able to create equality between myself as a leader in the facility and those in non-leadership positions.

OPEN BODY LANGUAGE TO CREATE A POSITIVE ENVIRONMENT

I constantly reminded myself to maintain open body language. I made a conscious effort not to cross my arms or put my hands in my pocket. I always made sure that my shoulders, hips, feet pointed in the direction of the person that I was speaking with.

My desire was that everyone I spoke with knew that they had my undivided attention. I constantly reminded myself of the corner stone principles that I spoke about in the first three chapters of the book. Everyone desires to be liked, understood and heard.

Verbal synchronization played an important part in being able to build rapport with people who spoke differently than I spoke. I remember a nice lady who was from New York City. She spoke a lot faster and a lot louder than I spoke, I immediately adjusted my pace and volume to match hers. As the conversation continued I noticed that when we first start speaking her body language was tensed and she wasn't facing me or making much eye contact while we were speaking. After a few minutes into the conversation I had completely synchronized my tone of voice and volume with hers. Following the synchronization almost instantly her body language completely changed. She was making great eye contact and her shoulders knees and toes where pointing completely in my direction. By the time I had left to go to my office we were both laughing and smiling and I had given her a number of high fives.

TECHNIQUES I USED TO BUILD RAPPORT

- After saying hello I Verbally Synchronized.
  (Michael Ellisberg)

- Match their Communication Style
  (Terry Mahoney)
  Kinesthetic
  Auditory
  Visual

- While the other person was speaking I made sure that I was smiling and nodding, allowing them to know that I was engaged in our conversation. Smiling is recognized around the world as a sign of happiness. (Daniel Nettle)

I reminded myself that everyone desires to be liked, heard, and understood. I found something that I liked about them, maybe it was their hair cut or maybe it was how well they were doing their job. I made sure to let them know that I felt that they were doing an awesome job and told them that we appreciated how well they did their job. I asked if they had any concerns or if they did something different that could benefit others. I let them know that I understood how valuable and important they were to the company. (David J. Lieberman)

ACTIONS SPEAKS LOUDER THAN WORDS

With the new bond created between the staff and myself, I was able to focus on rebuilding the relationship between the facilities and the different businesses, organizations, and companies that could provide patients for our skilled nursing and rehabilitation center.

As I was rebuilding the reputation in the community, it caused me to focus on how people saw me while I was out in the community. I had to have the highest level of professionalism. I also had to display a level of confidence in myself and in the facility I was representing. There were a number of techniques that I used to help show that I was confident and professional:

TECHNIQUES THAT I USED TO DISPLAY CONFIDENCE:

- Straight posture: standing straight with correct posture can make you look ten pounds lighter and helps you to look long and lean. (Shelly Hagen)

- Make strong eye contact: hold eye contact for 2-3 seconds. I wanted people to understand that I was proud of where I worked and confident and honest. (Michael Ellisberg)

- Be the first person to initiate a hand shake. (Linda Lee)

- Say hello with a smile: I said hello to everyone that I made eye contact with; my desire was for people to know that I was a very happy and friendly person. When I spoke with people I constantly smiled, even as they spoke. (Daniel Nettle)

- Touch- touching someone on the arm or shoulder to build rapport especially while saying their name. (Allan Pease)

- Speak loud and clear- One of my mentors told me that "the only person that doesn't speak up is someone who doesn't want to be heard or is hiding something." By speaking loud and clear, I was able to set myself apart from other marketers. (Terry Mahoney)

- Ask questions-Why, when, where, how- Find out as much as you can about the person that you are speaking with. (Terry Mahoney)

- Hands are relaxed, at the sides, or on the table. (Linda Lee)

- Face is relaxed. (Russell and Fernandez-Dols)

- Dress Professionally. (Susan Bixler & Nancy Nix-Rice)

- Walk quickly-One of the first ways to tell how a person feels is to watch how they walk. I walked as a man with a purpose. I didn't drag my feet as though I was tired, but I walked with a bounce in my step. Very energetically. (Allen Pease)

- Synchronize their open gestures-Arms and legs not crossed, clothing is likely to hang loosely, jacket not buttoned completely or top button on your shirt unbuttoned for men or women. Not holding anything in front of you (example: a glass of water or a book or clip board). (David J. Lieberman)

In a very short time, the reputation of the facility had completely changed. When people thought about my facility they thought about me and how professional and confident I was. Within thirty days the amount of referrals increased. After forty-five days we were competing with the larger and newer facilities. A little less than sixty days we were at capacity and our reputation in the community was greatly improved 100% and I knew that my knowledge of communication played a large part both with the staff that I worked with and the decision makers in the community.

<u>TECHNIQUES TO REMEMBER</u>

Techniques I used to Help Create Equality

- Open Body Language(Allan Pease)
  - Make a conscious effort not to cross your arms or put your hands in your pockets.

- Physical Touch
  - High fives, pat on the back, hand hug

- Synchronize your speech with theirs. (Ian R. McLaren)

- Match their communication style (Terry Mahoney)
  - Kinesthetic
  - Auditory
  - Visual

- Smiling is recognized around the world as a sign of happiness. (Daniel Nettle)

CHAPTER FIFTEEN
WINNING COMMUNICATION FOR LEADERS

After a number of years of successful marketing and improving immensely the reputation of two community facilities, I was extremely fortunate to land one of my all time dream jobs. I accepted the position as the Director of Operations (DOO) of a newly started medical group that focused on family practice and urgent care.

This was my first experience of running the operations of any company and I was bursting with excitement and nervousness. I remember my first day as DOO, I woke up around 2:00 a.m. and walked around my house practicing how I was going to say hello to everyone as I walked into the office and what I would say in our first morning meeting. Between the hours of 2:00 a.m. and 6:00 a.m., I did over five hundred push-ups and sit-ups, which was something I did whenever I was feeling nervous.

THE ART OF COMMUNICATION

My nervousness increased when I learned about all of the paperwork and reading I was going to encounter. I asked myself is this too much for a person with dyslexia? I remember feeling my heartbeat increase in speed; it felt like my heart was going to beat out of my chest. The faster my heart would beat the more push-ups I would do. I knew that exercise was a great way to release endorphins which would help reduce my stress and nervousness.

As the time drew closer for me to leave for work, I remembered how it felt the first day I had to go to the special education classroom after finding out that I had dyslexia. I remember feeling like I was a dumb loser, walking to that special class. I stared into the small windows of the regular classes watching as the other students laughed and talked with one another, and I felt that they were all laughing at me. As I walked into the special education classroom, none of the students were talking or laughing. I sat down at my assigned seat. My back pack felt like it was full of bricks. To this day that was the second longest day of my life; the longest day was when I woke up that morning to start as DOO.

While I was driving to the office, I pulled over and grabbed my journal from my briefcase and started writing all of the names of people who had been my personal cheerleaders and had supported me throughout the years: my mother, father, sisters, brothers, teachers, and friends. I also wrote down the different experiences I had as a horrible car salesman; how I felt overwhelmed working in the mortgage industry; and then the bad reputation of the skilled nursing facilities. I thought to myself, "All of these things turned out great even with my dyslexia." Reflecting on the hurdles from my past and how I overcame them really boosted my confidence. When I walked into the office, I felt like a king! I walked in with my shoulders back, head held high, and a bounce in my step.

The area where the office was located was full of endless possibilities, and it was my job as the face of the company to build a positive brand that represented the company's mission and vision. It was also my job to grow the name of the company in the community and to increase the number of patients.

Being a new company, I had to use cost effective marketing strategies, and to do this, I had to think outside of the box. I could have stuck to the traditional marketing and advertising strategies, and we would have experienced slow growth, but that wasn't what I had planned.

I knew that if we were going to have rapid growth in an industry where it wasn't common for people to change their physician, I was going to have to communicate to them in such a way that it would be in their best interest to use our services. The area was an extremely heavily populated Spanish speaking area, and I didn't allow the thought that I spoke very little Spanish to discourage me, I just reminded myself that non-verbal communication spoke louder than verbal.

My goal was to find ways to have face time with the local residents. During face time, I was able to speak face to face with residents of the community. This strategy was a more relational and cost effective way of marketing. I knew that I was not going to be able to see as many people if I just spent my money on sending out mailers or advertising in print media (news papers, billboards, or flyers).

My main marketing strategy was to do a door to door campaign, establishing deep relationships with the local businesses and to have a strong presence in the apartments that were in walking distance.

THE DOOR TO DOOR CAMPAIGN

I must admit going door to door even made me nervous. When I spoke with my colleagues regarding my endeavor they all suggested that I hang the information on the door, but I knew that I needed to meet people face to face. I felt that we were going to make a huge impact in the community, showing that we were there for them.

There were specific techniques I used when marketing door to door; these techniques displayed my openness. I wanted the person to know that I was open, sincere, and not trying to hide anything from them. The techniques were:

- **Limiting Moving My Hands**
  - When I first rang the door bell or knocked on the door, I stepped back to make sure that they could see all of me, whether they were looking through a peep hole or if they slightly opened the door. (Allan Pease)

  - As much as possible, I showed the palms of my hands while I was speaking.(Linda Lee)

  - While they were speaking I either kept my hands by my side or was holding my marketing material. If I needed to move my hands for any reason I would make sure to keep eye contact and move my hands slowly. (Linda Lee)

  - I tried my best to not touch my earlobe, my neck, or my nose. My desire was to show the person that I was being honest; these body parts are places on the body that people either rub on for comfort or scratch. Touching those specific parts of your body communicates deception. (Elizabeth Kuhnke)

- **Genuine Smile**
  - o I made sure that I showed my teeth.(Elizabeth Kuhnke)
  - o Relaxed my face. .(Elizabeth Kuhnke)

- **Smiled with My Eyes**
  - o Lifted my eyebrows (Michael Ellisberg)
  - o Raised my cheekbones (Daniel Nettle)
  - o Relaxed my face (Daniel Nettle)

- **My Shoulders, knees, and feet were pointing directly in their direction.**
  - o I wanted to make sure that the person knew that they had my complete attention and I was interested in whatever they had to say. (Shelly Hagen)

I wish I could say that every time I went to someone's door, they opened it and I was able to tell them about our wonderful services, but that was not what happened in the beginning. One of the very first doors I knocked on was an elderly Hispanic gentleman who was extremely hard of hearing.

When I first knocked on his door I was super excited. After knocking, I took two steps back so that he could see me fully and after waiting for a few minutes and no response, I decided to knock again because I could hear someone walking around inside. So I knocked again and took two steps back, and still no answer. This time I didn't hear anyone walking around, but I did hear the television channels being changed.

At this time, my frustration level had gotten to a point where it was hard for me to even smile. I didn't want to give up! I told myself, "I'm going to try one last time." I knocked harder than before, but I wasn't disrespectful. I took two steps back and waited patiently. I then saw a nice, older gentleman peeking through the window curtains. As soon as I saw his face, I noticed that he was wearing hearing aids, so it made sense to me why he was not answering. I waved and smiled as he looked out the window, he yelled at me "Go away!" So I placed the information on the door handle.

Marketing door to door was the hardest type of selling I had ever experienced. When I sold cars people had negative opinions of car salesmen, but they still needed to purchase a car. But to go door to door to someone's living room was truly difficult. I was able to stay focused by reminding myself that the information I was promoting was going to add value to the health and well being of the people in that community. I had to remind myself, non-stop, not to take it personally. I just had to find a better way to communicate the information. I felt I only needed one person to really listen to me, and towards the end of my first day of going door to door, I was granted that wish. I had the encounter I needed to encourage and remind me that my marketing strategy was the best one for our young company.

Even though I had a number of people to turn me down, I made sure that my body language was positive. Having positive body language helped me to have a positive attitude. I noticed that when I first left the office that morning I was extremely excited and I was smiling and laughing, but as more people were telling me "no" over and over again, my attitude became less positive, which showed through my body language.

MY NEGATIVE BODY LANGUAGE WAS DEMONSTRATED IN THE FOLLOWING WAYS:

- I didn't walk with a bounce in my step. I walked very slow and dragged my feet.
- A few times my hands were in my pockets or crossed.
- It was hard for me to make eye contact with people when they told me that they weren't interested.

Chapter Fifteen

During my lunch break I knew that I needed to redirect my thinking, so I listened to Brain Tracy's, *Psychology of Selling* to help me think positively. I sat in my car for ten minutes looking in the mirror saying, "I like myself, I love myself, and I'm going to do great!"

At the end of the day, I had an encounter with a nice, middle class lady with three children. When I knocked on her door, I did the following: I took two steps back; made sure that I had the palm of my hands up to show that I had nothing to hide; my shoulders were back; and I had a warm genuine smile on my face. While telling her my name and the name of the company, I was nodding my head, gesturing to her subconsciously that everything was okay. After I finished telling her my name and the services we provided, she told me that her husband had recently lost his job and they didn't have insurance. They could not afford the high cost of private insurance; however, their children were able to receive Medicaid through the state. We sat down in their living room and I was able to share with them my companies' desire, which is to help those who are not able to afford health care services. As I was speaking with them I made sure that my body language was a certain way:

- I was the first person to offer my hand to shake hands, I used the upper handshake. (Allan Pease)

THE ART OF COMMUNICATION

- I had proper posture- showing them that I was listening and focused completely on what they were saying.

- I sat on the edge of my seat with my feet flat on the floor. I wanted them to know that I was engaged in the conversation.

- I made sure that I was using my hands as I was speaking, to show that I was comfortable with what I was talking about.

- I used positive eye contact, making sure that I was making eye contact with both the husband and the wife. (Michael Ellisberg)

- I relaxed my face. I did not want to show tension or stress so I made sure that my face was relaxed. As I listened and nodded my head, conveying that I was following the conversation.
(Paul Ekman Ph. D)

- I informed them of how we could help them as I was speaking I placed my right hand over my heart (to show them that I was speaking from my heart), and lowered my hand with my palm opened, and directed my hand towards them. It was my desire to let them to know that we were passionate about helping people going through hard times. (Linda Lee)

- I listened to their communication style so that I could build verbal rapport with them. (Michael J. Losier)

When I informed them of how affordable our services were, their body language completely changed from negative to positive. They both started smiling, I watched as their shoulders went from being tensed to relaxed and their breathing pattern slowed down. The wife uncrossed her arms and she was no longer looking at her husband from the side when he was talking, but she turned and faced him so that her body was now turned towards him.

The husband's body language also dramatically changed. At first I noticed negative body language in his face, hands, arms, and in his feet. When his wife first told me that he lost his job and was no longer employed, he crossed his arms and slowly shifted his body away from the direction we were sitting. I also noticed that he tightened his jaw and he started breathing noticeably faster. Every time his wife mentioned that their children were on Medicaid, he immediately started slowly tapping his feet and rubbing his hands.

- Crossing his arms suggested that he was closed off and wasn't in agreement with what was being said. (Shelly Hagen)

- Slowly shifting his body suggested that he didn't want to face what he was going through.(Brook S. Edward M.D)

- Tightening his jaw implied that he was trying to control his emotions. (Elizabeth Kuhnke)

- Rubbing the back of his neck told me that the conversation was painful. (Allan Pease)

- Placing his finger across his lips told me that he desired to speak. When I noticed him doing that, I asked for his feedback. (Linda Lee)

Very little eye contact-when he did look at me and when we did connect eye to eye, he would immediately look down and to the right. This let me know that he felt some shame and guilt. (Russell and Fernandez-Dols)

When we were coming to the end of our conversation we were all smiling and laughing; their negative body language became positive, and I even made them a appointment to have a wellness visit the very next week. Before I left, I asked them both if any of their neighbors were in similar situations and could benefit from the affordable services from my company. They wrote me a long list of family and friends who all lived in that area and the wife even called them to tell them that I was going to meet with them.

Being able to read the negative gestures that both the husband and wife were displaying helped me to truly connect and build a deep bond. I wanted them to know that I was truly listening and that I honestly cared about what they were going through.
Many of the people in that area spoke little to no English, but being able to use proper body language allowed me to bridge the language gap and help people feel comfortable speaking with me even though I was a complete stranger.

BUSINESS TO BUSINESS RELATIONSHIPS

Going into a local business and trying to build rapport is a little difficult when your goal is not to purchase anything from them, but to sell them your services. During my first few business encounters, I brought packs of gum as a cover-up and then tried to educate them about my company's services; however, the conversations never lasted long since they viewed me as a customer and not a mutual businessman, trying to grow in the same surrounding area. I quickly changed my approach, keeping in mind that my goal was to build strong rapport with all local businesses and find out how we could help each other. I needed to demonstrate confidence, professionalism, and knowledge of my product. It was important that I displayed body language that would allow the business owners to know that we were both equal to one another.

The area businesses were very culturally diverse, so I needed to make sure that I was not being offensive with my verbal or non-verbal language.

In Western cultures, eye contact and physical contact are regarded differently than the Far East. My first diverse encounter was when I walked into a business and the owner was Japanese. I reached out to shake his hand and he softly shook my hand. The conversation was very short and he quickly, but nicely, let me know that he wasn't interested. As soon as I sat in my car, I realized my huge mistake was reaching out to shake his hand. I should have waited to see if he was going to raise his hand or respectfully bow.

Body Language with Far Eastern Cultures:
- Hands and Arms (Roger E Axtell) Shaking hands or touching is a sign of disrespect.
    - When I met with business owners, I made sure that I did not raise my hand to shake theirs unless they raised their hand first. I would respectfully nod my head.

- o While speaking I would not use arm gestures, but I would keep my arms by my side.

- o I would not make physical contact.

- Feet (Elizabeth Kuhnke) Feet are thought as being very dirty.

- o I made sure that my feet were flat on the floor and that the soles of my shoes didn't show.

- o Didn't place my feet on any furniture.

- Eye Contact (Roger E Axtell) Making strong eye contact shows lack of respect.

- o I did not make eye contact with them unless they were consistently making eye contact with me.

- My Shoulders and Hips (Roger E Axtell) Showing humility is very important.

- o I pulled my shoulders forward to make them seem smaller, which is a gesture of humility.

- o My hips and shoulders were never completely turned and were slightly to the side of who I was speaking with.

Body Language with Western Cultures:
- Hands and Arms (Linda Lee) Shows that you are confident and comfortable.
  - When I met with business owners, I made sure to raise my right hand to shake hands.

  - I would use my hands to make physical contact (touch on the shoulders, arm or pat on the back).

  - Use my hands as I was speaking.

- Eye Contact (Shelly Hagen) Shows that you are respectful and being honest.
  - Strong eye contact to builds trust and establishes rapport.

- Shoulders and Hips (Allan Pease)
  - My shoulders and hips turned to the direction of the person I was speaking with.

  - Shoulders were pulled back to show that I was confident.

Taking the time to understand how each culture communicates helped me to build rapport with the different business owners in the area. There were times that I made some mistakes, but because I was willing to adapt my way of communicating to other customs and cultures, I was able to build instant rapport and show that I had respect for them and their culture.

The most successful experience I had while marketing business to business was from a Thai restaurant owner. I stopped by the large Thai restaurant, located a few blocks from my office. I walked in and asked if the owner was in and the lady told me yes that he was in his office in the back. I asked her if I could meet with him. She walked me to his office in the back and as I stepped into his office, he was seated behind his desk. As I walked into his office he stayed seated, I slightly nodded my head and then said hello and told him my name and the name of my company. I made very little eye contact and kept my arms to my side as I was speaking.

I was standing there for about three to five minutes telling him about the services we provide. Every few seconds I would glance up to make sure that he was still paying attention. After informing him of our services, I asked him if he had any questions and then I stopped speaking. I stood there for a few seconds, but it seemed like years, and he suddenly asked if we gave flu shots? I answered yes! I had to catch myself, making sure I synchronized my tone, volume, and the pace of my speaking with his. I didn't want to break the rapport we established. I knew that because he asked that question, he was interested. He then informed me that he didn't provide insurance to his employees, but he would allow me to place our information in the break area and that he would also let them know that we provide flu shots. I thanked him for his time, and as I was about to leave his office he stood up and placed out his hand for me to shake. He did not shake my hand as firm as someone from the Western culture, but he did place his full hand in the palm of my hand and he made eye contact as he shook my hand. As he made eye contact I made sure to look at him in his eyes and then looked down to make sure that he knew that I respected his cultural gestures.

A few days after visiting with the Thai restaurant owner, I was working in my office and walked to the front desk to fax some documents and I noticed one of his employees and her entire family. Later that day one of the medical assistant that worked at the front desk knocked on my door to inform me that someone was there to see me. When I walked out to the front lobby, I saw that it was the family I spoke with in their living room, about our services. They told me that they had made us their primary physician for their entire family and that all their friends and their family members would also start coming to our office. That was great news! But the best news was that husband had recently started working for a local company as a maintenance technician!

While walking back to my office one of the medical assistants asked me if the family was old friends of mine or if they attended church with me. I laughed and told her that they were one of the families that I met while I was walking door to door. She said that she thought that I had been friends with them for years by the way we spoke to one another.

A year after working as Director of Operations, the amount of patients in our company had grown. In the beginning, we were seeing from one to five patients daily and it increased to twenty-five to thirty-five patients daily. We had established a strong reputation with all of the local business, schools, and state agencies. Our physicians were regarded to be some of the most respectable physicians in Dallas, Texas.

I would never take complete credit for the rapid growth of any of the companies I was a part of. To be honest, I was never the smartest or the most educated person anywhere I worked, but for me, developing my knowledge of how people communicated played a substantial part in my success.

When I decided to resign as the Director of

Operations of the medical group to focus on my career as a Body Language Expert and a Communications Coach, I read through my journals and thought about my educational journey in non-verbal and verbal communication and the massive amount of information that I was blessed to learn and apply to my personal and professional life.

I replayed the video of my life and reflected on my learning struggles in school; finding out that I had Dyslexia and Attention Deficit Disorder (ADD); and being placed in a special education classroom. Some people might think that it would be impossible to go from sitting in a special education classroom in the seventh grade to one day being the Director of Operations of a company. I would have to say that if a person thinks that it is impossible then it will be impossible, but I have always been blessed to have people in my life that believed in me and saw the best in me, even when I didn't see it in myself.

To succeed you must first improve, to improve you must first practice, to practice you must first learn, and to learn you must first fail."

Wesley Woo

TECHNIQUES TO REMEMBER

- Crossing your arms suggest that you are closed off and not in agreement with what is being said. (Shelly Hagen)

- Slowly shifting your body suggests that you don't want to face what you are going through. (Brook S. Edward M.D)

- Tightening your jaw implies that you are trying to control your emotions. (Elizabeth Kuhnke)

- Rubbing the back of your neck tells me that the conversation is painful. (Allan Pease)

- Placing your finger across your lips tells me that you desire to speak. When I noticed that, I ask for feedback. (Linda Lee)

- Very little eye contact-Not looking at the person and looking down and to the right, tells me that there are some feelings of shame and guilt. (Russell and Fernandez-Dols)

WORK CITED

- Roshan Cools, Journal of Cognitive Neuroscience, MIT Press Journal. October 2004 Posted Online March 13, 2006.
- Rim Dumbar, Neuroscience and Bio behavioral Reviews Volume 34, Issue 2, February 2010, Pages 260-280 Touch, Temperature, Pain/Itch and Pleasure.
- Brooks S. Edwards, M.D. Mayo Clinic Staff, Depression and anxiety: Exercise eases symptoms. Mayo Clinic Medical News letter 2001.
- Shelly Hagen, The Everything Body Language Book, 2nd Edition, Succeed in work, love, and life—all without saying a word! 2001
- Russell and Fernandez-Dols, eds..The Psychology of Facial Expression1997.
- David J. Lieberman, Get Anyone To Do Anything 2000.
- Dr. Bart Bishop, How to Increase Dopamine Release-Pain.com April 20, 2011.
- Linda Lee, The Hand Book, Interpreting handshakes, gestures, power signals and sexual signs.
- Allan Pease, The Definitive Book of Body Language.
- Daniel Nettle, Happiness: The Science behind Your Smile.
- Shlomo Vaknin, NLP for Beginners: Only The Essentials.

- Michael Hall Ph D, Mind Lines: Lines for Changing Minds.
- Ian R. McLaren, Communication Excellence: Using NLP to Supercharge Your Business Skills.
- Paul Ekman Ph. D Emotions Revealed.
- Terry Mahoney Making You Words Work: Using NLP to Improve Communication, Learning & Behavior.
- Susan Bixler & Nancy Nix-Rice, The New Professional Image: Dress Your Best for Every Business Situation (2nd Edition)
- Paul Ekman Ph. D and Wallace V. Friesen, Unmasking the face: A Guide to Recognizing Emotions from Facial Expressions.
- Michael Ellisberg, The Power of Eye Contact: Your Secret for Success in Business, Love and Life.
- Dr Stephan Juan, The Odd Body
- Michael J. Losier, Law of Connection
- Elizabeth Kuhnke, Body Language for Dummies.
- Roger E Axtell, Gestures: the Do's and Taboo of Body Language Around the World

YOHANCE PARKER'S MOST REQUESTED TOPICS

Communication
"*Winning Communication for Leaders*"
"*Sale Like a Rock Star with Effective Communication*"
"*ABC's of Customer Service*"

Sales Training
"*Health Care Sales Training*"
"*Selling with Integrity*"
"*Close More Now!!*"

Team Building and Workshops
"*IMPACT*"
"*All for One and One for All*"
"*Leap*"

Motivational
"*Seeing Past Your Now*"
"*The Secret to Get Anyone to Say Yes!*"
"*You Can Be A World Changer*"

"Great Book! I will definitely be able to apply lots of the techniques you have shared. Body language and communication are huge in my industry. I don't have any face to face conversations, so being able to read them and adjust to what their body language is saying is a MUST!"

Lina Hart
DJ (www.artistecard.com/djlinahart)

"Great personal stories with practical application techniques that tie in to create an awesome communication guide"

Jennifer Onwumere
Principal/Founder
Jen-Gerbread Marketing

"Mr. Yohance Parker diagnosed with 'Attention Deficit Disorder' and Dyslexia, at a young age, has written an exciting book on 'The Art of Communication." This gift from Mr. Parker to the world shows us how to overcome barriers to effective communication. It challenges and shows us how to use the magic of our body language to effect great communication and reap the benefits. I highly recommend it."

Daniel Jingwa
Author, Blue Sky Thinking

"Yohance uses real life experiences and powerful techniques to help the reader to be able to instantly apply great information and I've noticed an increase in my confidence and success with my clients."

Paul O'Neal
Vice President of Public Relations
SD&F Advertising, Inc

In a time when technology seems to have replaced the "human" element in communication, The Art of Communication affirms the vital importance of genuinely connecting with others. In a hands-on and practical manner, Yohance has captured the one thing that drives us all, relating and influencing others".

Jacob Akers
Licensed Clinical Counselor